Alternatives in
Jewish Bioethics

SUNY Series in Jewish Philosophy

Kenneth Seeskin, Editor

Alternatives in
Jewish Bioethics

Noam J. Zohar

State University of New York Press

Published by
State University of New York Press, Albany

For information, address State University of New York Press,
State University Plaza, Albany, N.Y. 12246

Production by M. R. Mulholland
Marketing by Nancy Farrell

Library of Congress Cataloging-in-Publication Data

Zohar, No' am.
    Alternatives in Jewish bioethics / Noam J. Zohar.
        p.   cm. — (SUNY series in Jewish philosophy)
    Includes bibliographical references and index.
    ISBN 0-7914-3273-4 (hc : alk. paper). — ISBN 0-7914-3274-2 (pb :
alk. paper)
    1. Medicine—Religious aspects—Judaism. 2. Bioethics.
3. Medical laws and legislation (Jewish law) 4. Ethics, Jewish.
I. Title. II. Series.
BM538.H43Z64 1997
296.3'85642—dc20   96-17494
                                                      CIP

10 9 8 7 6 5 4 3 2 1

Contents

Acknowledgments

The dialogue between the Jewish and Western traditions, of which this book forms a part, has been central to my consciousness from early adolescence onwards. It is a tribute to my parents, Yitzhak Zohar and Ora (Levin) Zohar, that they succeeded in fostering a home ambience of rich pluralism and strong commitments. Building on that foundation, God has granted me the chance to learn from many mentors. My initial training in Talmud was with Rabbi Shimon Friedlander, erstwhile of the Mir Yeshiva in Lithuania, and in the Socratic method, during those same years, from my brother Zvi Zohar in countless dialogues.

My Talmudic skills were further honed during my years at Yeshivat Hakotel in Jerusalem. Above all, I have benefited from the many sessions with my study partner (havruta) Hayyim Sabato. I pursued further Judaic and philosophical studies at the Hebrew University and the Shalom Hartman Institute (SHI) in Jerusalem. I have learned greatly from Professors David Hartman and David Heyd.

It was at the SHI, with its atmosphere of intensive commitment and exploration, that my interest in bioethics was first kindled. For several years the SHI sponsored an on-premises working group on Jewish bioethics. I wish to thank the various members of that group, with whom I initially investigated many of the issues in this book. In addition, I wish to especially thank SHI director David Hartman for many hours of quality Torah study and for his continued faith in my work. To the American and Canadian Friends of the SHI, and especially to the late Saul Lederman zal and, yibadel lehayim, Bob Kogod, goes my gratitude for their generous support over the years, which has made this work possible.

Over the past few years I have had the privilege of discussing in numerous settings the materials and ideas explored below. This was done most extensively in seminar meetings at the School of Social Sciences, Institute for Advanced Study at Princeton, and in the annual meetings of the Oxford-Princeton-Mt. Sinai Bioethics Consortium, headed by Dr. Rosamond Rhodes. I wish to thank participants in all these meetings for their many insightful comments and critiques.

I have learned abundantly from my students, first in Religion 243 at Princeton University, and subsequently in various courses at Bar Ilan University. The Philosophy Department of Bar Ilan has encouraged my continued work on applied ethics in general and Jewish bioethics in particular.

Many people have devoted their time and wisdom to careful reading of my manuscript or parts thereof, offering fruitful comments and suggestions. Special thanks to Dr. Roger Crisp, Prof. Elliot Dorff, Prof. David Heyd, Dr. Menachem Lorberbaum, Prof. Jeff MacMahan, Prof. Ken Seeskin, Prof. Michael Walzer, Dr. Anat Zohar, and Dr. Zvi Zohar.

Finally, I wish to express my deepest thanks and love to my family for their patience and understanding through years of intensive work. For many stimulating philosophical conversations on various problems discussed below I extend my appreciation to my children Ohr, Rachelli, and Marva. And above all I thank my partner Anat for her warm support and encouragement throughout these many years of our joint journey. Long before applying her acute scientific reasoning to advise me on improving my explanations and arguments, her zest for life and her intellectual honesty have nourished me and my project.

Introduction

I. Can There Be "Jewish Bioethics?"

Some people wonder whether there can be "Jewish ethics." Their doubts cannot, however, be answered simply by an invitation to enter a library and note the various relevant titles, or by pointing to the vast tradition of Jewish normative discourse stretching back across three millennia. Although they recognize all this, their doubts persist, reflecting not a lack of information but reservations about basic premises.

These reservations converge, as it were, from both sides. On the one hand there is what I shall call the universalist objection. The universalist objection, which argues that "ethics" excludes any parochial hyphenation, will be examined in this section. On the other hand there is what I shall call the Divine Authority objection. In the name of divine authority, some scholars claim that "Jewish" precludes an attachment to critical moral deliberation. This objection will be addressed in section III below. Addressing each of these challenges in turn seems the best way to introduce the project of this book.

The universalist objection opposes any "particular ethics," whether Jewish, Islamic, Japanese, or French. The objection stems from a view of ethics as essentially universal in both scope and epistemic access. Basic moral judgments apply to all moral agents (=universal scope), and moral discourse consists precisely in employing a general human faculty of practical reasoning (=universal access). For example, it is wrong to torture people and right to rescue them from enduring pain. This is true with regard to all people, and it holds for all moral agents; it is not "Jewishly right" or "wrong for the French," just plain right and wrong for everyone toward everyone.

One impetus of this ethical universalism is the rejection of moral relativism. For the relativist, there is *nothing but* a set of autarchic cultural realms, and specifically no "bioethics" in general, but only "Jewish bioethics," "Japanese bioethics," etc. Against this, the universalist repudiates parochial norms, insisting instead on a common standard. For him, true moral discourse is to be distinguished by its universality, consisting, for example, in the formulation of general rules which apply to everyone everywhere;[1] any "X-ish Ethics" is in principle an oxymoron. There can be, then, no valid realm of Jewish bioethics, for as long as the discourse is particularly Jewish, it is outside the proper realm of ethics. As one author says,

> If we admit that the criterion of generality is fundamental to normative ethics then the concept of a parochial normative ethic must be illegitimate when considered in any but purely historical terms. (Kellner 1987, at 50)

Even on this view, an ethnic qualifier for "ethics" could be thought to apply in certain modest ways. I will examine two of these; the first, which is rather trivial, leads to the second, which is of greater significance. Together they serve to define the limits of "X-ish" ethics for a universalist.

First, it is possible—on account of either hereditary peculiarities or specific customs and norms of Jews' behavior—that medical care of Jews will sometimes involve unique problems. Where ethnic origins are, for example, genetically relevant to diagnosis or treatment, they must surely be given due attention, and conceivably, this might involve special (perhaps even unique?) moral issues. Discussion of such issues could, I suppose, count as "Jewish bioethics" in a marginal sense, but can be safely ignored in the present discussion.

Second, and more significant, would be cases where the special issues arise from specifically Jewish norms, such as those of the *Halakha*, the Jewish tradition of normative discourse.[2] For a person committed to such traditional norms, numerous conflicts or problems can arise in the context of medical practice. Perhaps the most common of these is the potential conflict with ritual observance of *shabbat* (=the Sabbath). The nature of the possible conflict can be appreciated by considering its specific elements.

Halakhic observance of the shabbat chiefly involves refraining from the "39 Crafts" (Mishna, *shabbat* 7:2). Examples of these would be lighting a fire (including the operation of an automobile engine) or writing (including that of a prescription). Although the shabbat prohibitions are explicitly suspended in life-threatening situations, not all medical settings are properly classified as involving an imminent threat to life, and complex problems can arise. The rules for "suspending shabbat for the sake of life-saving" have become the Halakhic paradigm for discussing conflicts between the requirements of vital emergencies and the prescriptions of everyday norms.[3]

Now what sort of problems and conflicts are these? On the above (universalist) conception of ethics, such dilemmas are not properly part of the realm of ethical discourse, since one of their horns is not truly "ethical": the shabbat obligations are patently not universal principles.[4] It follows that problems of this nature are best perceived from an internal perspective, that is, in the Jewish tradition's own terms. Within the Halakhic system, shabbat observance is obligatory, and this obligation might conflict with medical practice, which itself also embodies an obligation—that of "life-saving." This yields a conflict of obligations—a Halakhic dilemma, but no ethical dilemma.

True, an effort at generalization may yield an ethical question of the form: "In striving to fulfill the (universal) moral duties pertaining to medical practice, what weight should be given to personal commitments (of the patient and/or physician) where such commitments conflict with a medically prescribed course of action?" But then again, there is nothing specifically Jewish (or Catholic, or Chinese, etc.) in this question. It simply raises the serious problem of the place accorded to individual commitments and loyalties, or, to put it more strongly, to people's particular identities, within a universal framework of morality.

This brings to light what may be a fundamental flaw in the universalist orientation, namely, the fact that it would deny integration of such commitments into the body of moral obligations. This excludes from the realm of "morality" motives and reasons which people feel to be at the core of their personality. Such a rarified morality then runs the risk of substituting mere abstractions for the persons it purports to be addressing.[5]

This flaw may contribute to the fact that discussions of just such conflicts constitute a significant part of materials published under headings like "Medicine and Jewish Law." People committed to Halakha feel that some of their most pressing problems are left unmentioned in contemporary discussions of Bioethics and seek to supplement them with "Jewish bioethics," a realm which gives recognition to the special set of obligations to which they are committed.

But is it appropriate to call such discussions "bio*ethics*"? Clearly some traditional Jewish norms belong to the realm of ritual rather than to that of morality. Insofar as ramifications of such norms in medical settings are discussed under "Jewish bioethics," the caption "ethics" is indeed being wrongly extended to a parochial context. But what of Halakhic sources which address the moral realm? Should we grant the general exclusionary claim of the universalist objection, that ethical norms must be grounded in rational arguments outside of any particular tradition?

II. From Universalism to Pluralism

In fact, that universalist stance which would dismiss the voices of particular traditions in ethical discourse seems far from obvious. Indeed, it appears to involve a rather difficult demand, for where, outside of all particular traditions, is the desired general standard to be found? As heirs of the Enlightenment, we seek it in rational deliberation. But, although standards of rationality may suffice to exclude certain positions, they still leave us with a plurality of options. More than one perspective passes the threshold of rationality; many particular voices, embedded in various normative traditions, offer their disparate pronouncements of right and wrong, of good and evil.

In reality, there is no single system of universal ethics, abstracted from any (or from all) particular culture(s).[6] It is true that, pace relativist protests, moral judgments are addressed to all; morality is indeed universal in scope. But with regard to universal access, the picture is more complex. All people engage in moral judgments, but they do not share a uniform moral language; yet no particular tradition has a monopoly on universal truth. No specific moral tradition can lay an exclusive claim to embodying a general human faculty of practical reasoning. With regard to the source of our moral wisdom, we seem better advised to adopt some version of pluralism.

One such version would be *substantive pluralism*, the view that valid moral instruction is multifarious, that there is some validity in each of several incompatible positions. Such a stance is not without its problems, and I shall not try to defend it here. A more modest alternative is *procedural pluralism*, which amounts simply to a willingness to concede our limitations. With respect to any moral problem, there may in principle be a "truth of the matter," but all we possess are various discrete attempts to get at the right answer.

These brief observations hardly constitute, of course, an even minimally sufficient treatment of universalism, relativism, or pluralism. Indeed, my study of these theoretical frameworks did not precede, nor was it a precondition of, my engagement in the kind of investigations which constitute this book. The dialogue between distinct moral traditions documented in this volume is itself, if comprehensible, a document of (I think) some sort of pluralistic moral universe. I come to present the voices in dialogue, as I hear and understand them; let better theoreticians than I make meta-ethical sense of the conversation.

Assuming, then, pluralistic discourse as a central mode of moral philosophy, the notion of "Jewish bioethics" seems to make perfect sense. It should denote the contribution of the Jewish tradition to ethical discourse on medicine and human biology. Here, however, we encounter an opposite critique, advanced from the Jewish tradition's own (supposed) perspective, for, according to one view of this tradition, presenting claims grounded in Halakha as one voice within a common ethical discourse would be deeply misguided.

III. Divine Authority:
The Insular Conception of Halakha

For some authors in the field of Jewish bioethics, the particularist force of Halakhic commitment goes much further than the particularism suggested by our (above) notion of pluralism. Even when addressing common questions of bioethics, these writers either explicitly or implicitly represent their positions as grounded in the (divine) authority of received texts and of established precedents, to the exclusion of critical reasoning.

This perception of Halakhic discourse has given rise to some reservations about the very project of "Jewish bioethics." B. Brody, for instance, questions the "use of halakhic material as the basis for claims about the Jewish view on disputed topics in medical ethics." He argues that, as a rule, such material can only serve "as a basis for mandating certain forms of behavior for members of the Jewish faith who are perceived as bound by Jewish Law" (1983, at 319).

To my mind, however, Brody's point about the proper audience must lead to a more fundamental concern. If prescriptions derived from Halakhic sources hold no significance for people in general, why should even Jews be committed to follow them? One kind of answer is that a commitment to traditional Judaism consists precisely in accepting the complete authority of Halakhic pronouncements. This would appear to be anchored in a doctrine of divine command morality;[7] Halakha is viewed as the expression of God's revealed will, calling for obedience rather than ethical reasoning.

M. Graetz observes that such a view underlies some of the most prominent publications on Jewish Bioethics:

> When we examine existing treatments of this field, catalogued under the caption "Jewish Medical Ethics"—such as, e.g., the work of Jakobovits or Rosner—we find that nearly all of them merely report and expound precedents, citing *halakhic* rulings.[8]

For these authors, the commitment to Halakha—conceived as an insular realm of revealed law—seems to exclude any appeal to moral reasoning. As Graetz notes, this must be distinguished from proper ethical discourse, which necessarily involves "discussing ethical aspects of each decision, policy, and practice . . . including those whose origin is *Halakhic.*"

Thus Graetz, contrary to the authors he is criticizing, subscribes to a pluralistic conception of the origins of "ethical aspects": Halakha is but one among the pertinent normative sources. Yet he dubs their approach "classical," apparently accepting their depiction of Halakha as a formal system of authoritarian rulings. The primary alternative, he explains, consists in a "reformist" approach, which seeks to complement an essentially amoral Halakhic discourse by subjecting its conclusions to moral criticism.[9] Even the "reformists," however, share with authors of the "classical" school (and with critics like Brody) a view of Halakha as an insular, formal system bound by its own logic. Between ethics and Halakha there can be, on this view, no true dialogue.

The term "Jewish bioethics," then, signifies a project of accommodation aimed at resolving internal conflicts in the hearts of people with a dual allegiance—to (a supposedly universal) morality and to Halakha. This internal accommodation is akin to achievement of toleration between groups with distinct cultural identities. The goal in both cases is perceived in terms of peaceful coexistence; where no conflict arises, Halakha and ethics can contentedly each go its separate way. In case of conflict, where adherents of divine command morality would advocate obedience to God's command (as defined by Halakhic exposition), adherents of universal ethics will give precedence to the moral imperative.

IV. An Alternative View:
Halakhic Reasons and Moral Dialogue

But does the Halakhic tradition really have nothing to contribute to ethical discourse? In other words, is it true that this tradition cannot meaningfully speak other than in a voice of stark authority? D. Novak argues that, while this may be true regarding much of the Halakhic tradition, it is not true for all of it. Within Halakha, there is a core of norms akin to natural law, rationally grounded and conceived as universally binding. Novak finds this core in the seven "Noahide Laws," which, according to the Rabbis, apply to all humankind (all the "descendants of Noah"). These norms can be interpreted and applied through "Noahide reasoning," that is, ordinary rational discourse, as distinct from the special modes of argument (such as intricate scriptural hermeneutics) used in regular Halakhic discourse (Novak 1985).

Yet Novak seems to grant that, apart from this realm of "Noahide Reasoning," Halakhic argument is significant only for its adherents. They, who have accepted God's Torah, are obligated to follow its requirements as worked out through the special modes of Halakhic argument. In such (non-Noahide) Halakhic discourse, conclusions require, it is implied, neither more nor less than internal support through formal codes grounded in the system's authority. But that is, in fact, a wholly inadequate picture of the Halakha.

Historically, the Jewish normative tradition has rarely emphasized stark authority; rather, it has placed great emphasis upon the giving of reasons. This holds for the tradition's ancient roots in biblical law,[10] and is highly characteristic of the Talmud and of rabbinic Judaism generally.[11] Rules are explained and defined, traditions are variously interpreted and argued about—all in terms of their reasons.

The centrality of reasoning in the Halakhic tradition is reflected in the prevalence of rabbinic disagreements. The core document of the Rabbinic tradition, the Mishna, intentionally cites various opinions on myriad issues.[12] The pages of the Talmud, rabbinic Judaism's classical corpus, are filled with numerous and protracted arguments over the application and interpretation of virtually every law. This results directly from the fact that Halakhic arguments are not determined by formal deduction; the plurality of possible interpretations calls rather for moral reasoning and for judgments of value.

In contemporary discourse as well, authors grounded in the Jewish tradition hardly produce anything like a univocal representation of God's revealed will. In a detailed study focused on one question, life support for a dying patient, L. A. Newman (1990) has shown how the same body of received texts and precedents produces a great variety of conclusions through differences in text-selection and (even more important) in interpretations of the very same texts.

The choice which each author makes between alternative precedents and interpretations is not simply arbitrary. R. Green criticizes contemporary Halakhists for adopting especially "conservative" readings and interpretations of the tradition, which, he claims, sometimes go against basic values of the earlier Halakha. Through a series of examples, he argues regarding "some of the more salient writings in the area of Jewish bioethics today" that

> despite their authority and their erudition, these writings are not genuinely representative of the Jewish tradition as a whole. Not only the available secondary discussions of Jewish bioethics, but many of the contemporary Rabbinic discussions upon which they rest, display a markedly conservative tendency that is out of keeping with much of the spirit of the earlier tradition . . . (Green 1985, at 262)

Some of Green's examples are quite powerful; surely he adduces strong evidence that there is a tendency for one-sided representations in contemporary Jewish bioethics. But the characterization of these representations as "conservative" is too simple. It is true that the authors in question sometimes oppose particular novelties, but if they are opting against values well-documented in earlier sources, their stance is hardly conservative in the sense of "doggedly following received attitudes." In opposing such novelties, they are in fact opting *for* opposite values, probably also with deep traditional roots. Cutting through the authority-enhancing rhetoric which often claims to represent "*the* Jewish view," we should try to discern the particular valuations which would support each of two (or more!) rival interpretations.

Today, as in earlier periods, the argument for preferring one viable interpretation over another involves at least implicitly moral reasoning, which is part and parcel of all Halakhic discourse. True, the reasons are often quite different from those we might encounter in the discourse of Western ethics. The moral idiom, the values, the syntax— are hardly the same. Still, Halakhic discourse consists in moral reasoning, albeit coined in its own moral language. Halakha is, in the main, a system of religious ethics which can be brought into a dialogue with Western moral philosophy. Is not the whole point of pluralism that there can be a conversation among those who speak different languages?

V. Beyond Accommodation:
Translation and Intercultural Dialogue

In order to better understand the notion of a pluralistic moral conversation, let us again take up the analogy with the coexistence between two groups. Proponents of pluralism frequently voice hopes for something beyond mere toleration between cultural subgroups within a society. The different cultures are believed to promise each other mutual enrichment. Such a promise necessarily presumes the possibility of meaningful "translation," whereby a person belonging to one culture can truly appreciate and sometimes adopt elements of other cultures.[13] The goal is not, however, a totally homogeneous society, with the vari-colored several cultures finally merging into a uniform white haze. Infusions from other cultures are to be signifi-cant, else the promise of enrichment will be hollow, yet each culture is to retain its distinct integrity, shaping the incoming elements even as it is shaped by them.

Moreover, the image of completely distinct groups trad-ing in cultural elements is too simple, for in a pluralistic society, not every individual can be easily pigeonholed as "belonging" to precisely one culture. Mixed marriages, social interaction, the blessings of freedom of speech, and notably the express aims of a liberal-arts education are only some of the factors which are sure to produce people with double (or multiple) cultural allegiances.

For such people, mere intercultural translation, while essential in avoiding schizophrenia, is not enough. They need not strive for total integration, which (if attainable) would supposedly produce within an individual person a unique *sui generis* culture. Yet while within each person's world the several cultural components retain their distinct flavors and significance, there is likely to be a tendency toward finding a common denominator. Each set of norms embodies particular moral concepts and a moral vision of human existence and action. In the process of personal integration, the multiple concepts and visions get trans-lated back and forth and, it may be hoped, enhance each other, both positively (by providing new insights) and neg-atively (by inviting comparative criticism).

Implicit in this description of intercultural dialogue is a suggestion about the mode of translation. Forms of behavior, with their inherent potential for shaping our lives, serve as common currency. Addressed by both traditions, the same actions and ultimately the same character and biography are at stake.[14] When a concrete problem is illu-minated from different sources, it becomes a prism for mutual refraction. Hence the special relevance of an applied field like bioethics for intercultural dialogue.

This dual perspective characterizes the notion of "Jewish bioethics" central to this book—a distinct alternative to the insular approach more commonly represented as "Jewish bioethics." Implicit in this is an anti-authoritarian approach to Halakhic discourse, an openness to dialogue and criticism both internal and external, and the recognition that frequently there is no one true answer—nor even one uniform "Jewish answer"—to a given ethical problem. Therefore, we will be describing alternatives in another sense as well: on virtually all matters addressed below, we shall be exploring disparate and opposing views within the Jewish tradition.

Accordingly, the reader should be warned not to expect a definite resolution at the conclusion of each discussion or chapter. Although my personal views and attitudes are necessarily reflected in the choice of materials and in the way they are presented and analyzed, my purpose is not to rival the edicts of others by offering rulings of my own. Rather, it is to present alternative voices and sources, along with various possibilities of interpretation, from within the Halakhic tradition, and to promote a dialogue between these voices and contemporary voices in Western moral philosophy.

VI. The Structure of the Exploration:
Tracing the Divine

Our dual perspective determines also the organization of the project. The themes of the individual chapters will be familiar to anyone with an interest in bioethics: euthanasia (Chapter 2), new reproductive techniques (Chapter 3), triage (Chapter 4), constraints on medical research (Chapter 5), and social allocation of medical resources (Chapter 6). The approaches to the issues canvassed and analyzed here are Jewish first of all by virtue of their mode of discourse, which consists in applying and interpreting classical Jewish sources. But, as noted by E. Dorff (1991), we should also recognize a deeper influence of the Jewish tradition in the basic valuations and theological orientations which underlie and inform individual arguments and conclusions.

Specifically, the discussion here will focus on two core orientations: religious naturalism and religious humanism. Religious naturalism, as I use the term here, is an attitude that ascribes divine value to the world (or to certain of its features) as we find it. The results of God's work are believed to carry their own authority and should not lightly be tampered with. This is the main theme of Part I, comprising Chapters 1–3. The medieval debate over the basic legitimacy of medical intervention is analyzed at the outset, in Chapter 1. The next two chapters trace the ramifications of this debate regarding the issues of active euthanasia (Chapter 2) and of assisted (or "artificial") reproduction (Chapter 3). I aim to show how the basic debate over naturalism significantly illuminates the problematics of attributing authority to given facts, whether medical or social. Part I concludes on a skeptical note: the very enterprise of modern medicine is very hard to square with the quietistic tendency of religious naturalism.

From this discussion I move, in Part II, to a rather different religious emphasis, which holds greater overall prospects for fruitfully addressing contemporary concerns. This emphasis involves the Jewish version of religious humanism, centered on the idea of the divine image reflected in every human being. This idea is expressed in a high valuation of human life and even of the human body. I begin with a brief exposition of this idea as revealed in some classical rabbinic texts, followed by a detailed application on the micro level to the context of triage, where one human life must be balanced against another (Chapter 4) and on the macro level to the context of social allocation of scarce resources (Chapter 6). For reasons which will become clear, a discussion of limiting medical research out of respect for (dead) human bodies is interpolated (Chapter 5).

Altogether, I have not sought an exhaustive exploration of issues in contemporary bioethics, and more than one central question is not addressed here. In particular, I do not deal here with either the brain-death debate or the issue of abortion. The latter has been discussed rather extensively by Feldman (1974), and still, like other issues in Jewish ethics, awaits a full feminist analysis.[15] Rather, this work is intended to show how engaging fundamental religious values in dialogue with secular moral philosophy can help us in deciphering and judging the sense of many Halakhic arguments. The alternatives in Jewish bioethics, as presented here, are not a menu of competing authoritative statements, but voices in an intelligible discussion calling for understanding and for a considered response. As such, they should in turn make their own particular contribution to contemporary discourse in bioethics.

VII. A Note on Rabbinic Sources

Although Halakha is grounded in scripture (primarily in the Pentateuch, the five Books of Moses), the era of its classical development and formulation was post-biblical. This classical Rabbinic Period extended from the last few centuries of the Second Commonwealth (up to 70 C.E.) to the redaction of the Babylonian Talmud, around 500 C.E. The core of the talmudic corpus is the Mishna (edited by Rabbi Judah "the Prince," circa 200 C.E.), which collects the teachings of earlier sages under six "divisions," further divided by subject into tractates.

The Mishna faithfully but concisely records numerous disagreements; it generally omits, however, the reasons for rulings, both contested and unanimous. It is in the voluminous Talmud that Rabbinic debates are transmitted, refined, and carried forth with great intensity. Rabbinic Judaism henceforward is based on canonizing the Talmud with its complex dialectic form, where hardly any debate ends with a definite conclusion. There have been numerous codifications, notably including Maimonides's *Mishneh Torah* (="restatement of the Torah," twelfth century), Rabbi Jacob b. Asher's *'Arba'ah Turim* (="four columns," fourteenth century), and Rabbi Joseph Caro's *Shulhan 'Arukh* (="set table," sixteenth century). Still a crucial repository of Halakhic sources from both medieval and early modern times is the Responsa Literature, collections of reasoned rulings resembling court opinions, issued by eminent scholars in response to specific queries.

Citations from the Mishna or Talmud are given by tractate. For Mishnaic references, this is followed by two numbers separated by a colon, representing chapter and subsection (such as, *shabbat* 4:12); for talmudic references, by folio number and an indication of side (a or b, such as, *shabbat* 37a). Both these texts have been published in English translations, but the translations given here are my own, as are those of all other rabbinic materials, most of which have not been translated before.

The teachers of the classical (=talmudic) period are alluded to as "the Sages" or "the Rabbis" and their traditions as "Rabbinic." Lower-case "rabbis" or "rabbinic" are used generically for later (including contemporary) authors.

Notes

1. This was, of course, the impetus of Kant's categorical imperative; more recently, see Singer (1961).

2. For a general introduction to the Halakhic system and literature, see Elon (1994).

3. See Chapter 5 for an extensive example.

4. See Gereboff (1982), pp. 317 and 322 n6.

5. On this problem, see Sandel (1982).

6. And when it does appear to fit, it usually turns out that adherents of a particular tradition—say, Anglo-American liberalism—have simply mistaken their view for the rational approach; to them, its precepts seem self-evident!

7. For a discussion of the (rare) occurrence of this doctrine in earlier Jewish sources, and of reasons for its general rejection, see Sagi and Statman (1995).

8. Graetz (1991), at 80. For a detailed critique, along similar lines, of several prominent writers on Jewish bioethics, both Orthodox and Conservative, see Gereboff (1982).

9. Among practitioners of this approach, Graetz counts D.H. Gordis and D.B. Sinclair (ibid p. 81, n 3).

10. See, e.g., Walzer (1992).

11. See Weiss-Halivni (1986), a book whose subtitle is "the Jewish predilection for justified law" and Elon (1994), Chapter 7.

12. See Mishna *'eduyot* 1:5.

13. Regarding the feasibility of such translation, see L.A. Newman (1993). Newman still seems to accept something like Novak's distinction between two different strands or aspects of the Jewish tradition, only one of which has universal relevance.

14. Well, where there is any difference in the recommendations for action, it is not literally the *same* action which will be the subject of the disparate teachings. But from a logical point of view, insofar as each one of the instructions excludes the other, their referent is identical, since a in "not a" is identical to a in "a." A similar argument can be advanced regarding two prospective unfoldings of a person's biography, although it makes sense to ask, "If I consistently behave that way, won't I become a different person?"

15. In general, I have not, despite my own egalitarian tendencies, been able to draw on feminist voices in Jewish bioethics. Cf. Davis (1991), and more generally, Davis (1994).

PART I

Authority in Nature

1

Religious Naturalism:
Human Responsibility and Divine Decree

I. Intervention and Providence

Modern medicine is often at the forefront of techno-
logical advance, a triumph of applied empirical science.
Still, the goal of modern physicians is the same as that of
their less successful predecessors: overcoming injury and
illness. From a theistic perspective, this goal carries a
potential for tension with the demands of piety. Attempts
by human agents to heal the sick may appear to constitute
interference with divine plans.

The Jewish theistic tradition would seem especially
susceptible to such tension, for it combines a strong
emphasis on the duty to rescue any threatened human
being with a pervasive faith in divine providence. Amongst
the various sources of human suffering, illness—insofar
as it is not produced by human agency—is particularly
prone to be perceived as constituting divine chastisement,
as will be seen below.

An initial recognition of potential tension between
human responsibility and divine determination seems to
underlie a well-known talmudic statement about the "permission to heal." This "permission" is derived from a law in
Exodus 21:19, which stipulates that an assailant must
(among other liabilities) pay for his victim's healing:

"and he shall cause him to be thoroughly healed"—
this implies that a physician is granted permission to
heal. (BT, *bava qama* 85a).

The logic of this inference is simple: if the Torah—God's law—requires hiring a physician, then the physician's work cannot be illegitimate! D. Hartman sees in this text an endorsement of "[taking h]uman responsibility for the conditions of life." Medical practice represents human action in general: "The permission granted to the physician to heal signifies the legitimacy and importance of acting to alleviate human suffering." (Hartman 1985, 229–30). Such permission is needed because the existing state of affairs, along with the suffering it entails, is thought to be determined by God.[1] Why, then, is the physician's intervention appropriate? The Talmud simply pronounces it so, without offering any theological account.

The theological problem is openly confronted in an early medieval rabbinic discourse which draws an analogy between medical practice and other forms of human action—in the face of conditions produced by God. In the following text, two great rabbis are depicted both as physicians and as explicators of what might be termed "medical theology":

R. Ishmael and R. Akiva were strolling in the streets of Jerusalem accompanied by another person. They were met by a sick person. He said to them, "My masters, tell me by what means I may be Healed." They told him, "Do thus and so and be healed." He asked them, "And who afflicted me?" They replied, "The Holy One, blessed be He." [The sick person] responded, "You intrude in a realm which is not yours; He has afflicted and you heal! Are you not transgressing His will?"

They asked him, "What is your occupation?" He answered, "I am a tiller of the soil and here is the sickle in my hand." They asked him "Who created the orchard?" He answered, "the Holy One, blessed be He." Said they, "You too intrude in a realm which is not yours. [God] created it and you cut away its fruit!." He said to them, "Do you not see the sickle in my hand? If I did not plow, sow, fertilize and weed it nothing would grow." They said to him, "Oh you fool! Does your occupation not teach you this, as Scripture says 'as for man, his days are as grass: as grass of the field, so he flourishes' (Psalms 103:15). Just as a tree, without weeding, fertilizing and plowing will not grow; and even if it grows, then without irrigation and fertilizing it will not live but will surely die—so it is with regard to the body. Drugs and medical procedures are the fertilizer, and the physician is the tiller of the soil."[2]

But are plants which require cultivation a proper analogue to sick people in need of medical aid? With respect to agricultural activity, it can perhaps be supposed that God initially created the botanical realm intending for humans to realize its potential. In order to yield bountiful fruit, plants naturally require tending. But people's natural condition is, arguably, good health; they were not created needing medical treatment. If they fall from good health, is this not a direct result of divine will, which ought not to be countered by medical intervention?

This may invite a distinction between ailments according to their origin. For under the doctrine of free will, the acts of human agents, freely chosen, are not to be attributed to divine providence. So with regard to a person injured by the wicked—say, "God's enemies"—a healer could rather easily be perceived as doing God's work. But the sick are, surely, suffering by divine decree; how can there be permission to heal them?

D.M. Feldman plausibly employs this distinction in interpreting the teaching of Bahye ben Asher (Spain, thirteenth century), who writes[3] that the physician's license to heal does not extend to internal medicine. On this view, the "permission to heal" is restricted to humanly induced wounds, while organic pathologies are "presumed to be manifestations of divine rebuke or punishment and only God may heal or remove them."[4]

This position must have appeared radically pious even in the middle ages. In modern society, with the great success and wide acceptance of medical intervention, this view and the theistic consciousness it represents may appear totally anachronistic. Seeking to minimize the scope of ailments barred to human intervention, M. Weinberger[5] has proposed two restrictive interpretations of the medieval opposition to the healing of ailments "induced by God."[6] First, he plausibly points out that some "internal ailments" are in fact induced by human actions, including the patient's own actions, such as, unhealthy eating. If this is granted, then the class of God-induced ailments consists of only "a congenital illness, or one resulting from the body's weakness and sensitivity, or from the weakness and disfunction of particular organs."[7]

Weinberger's second restriction, put forward somewhat tentatively, is that "any illness whose nature and cure are clear, is not considered an `internal illness induced by heaven'; that term refers only to an illness whose nature is unclear, where the cure consists in nothing but groping and experimenting." The theological basis for this distinction is not explained; possibly the idea is that only events whose causal explanation evades us are ascribed to the realm of divine providence. In another vein, Weinberger notes that attempts to cure a mysterious illness are risky; they might cause more harm than benefit, and are thus best left to God. Medical intervention is permitted only on the basis of "certain knowledge." As noted by M. Halperin,[8] the notion of certain knowledge seems, however, naive and requires some explication, since "medicine never offers certain knowledge."

These efforts at ingenious reinterpretation reflect a wish to reconcile deep theological misgivings about medicine with the mainstream endorsement of medical intervention. But contemporary Halakhists have generally resisted even such minor exclusions from the license to heal. This resistance has not, however, been accompanied by a rejection of the mode of discourse which would attribute illness to divine causation. Belief in the divine authorship of illness continues to imply a fundamental theological challenge to all medical practice.

From this religious perspective, illness and medicine seem to present us with divine cross-purposes: the physician is allowed by God to compete, as it were, against His own work.[9] Although the physician's vocation is thus depicted as legitimate and even heroic, there seem to be grounds for worrying about overstepping legitimate boundaries. No moral system, of course, will mandate all medical activities without limits. But a physician working under divine dispensation might need to be concerned not only about the rights or interests of his or her patient (or those of third parties), but also about possible terms and conditions of the divine license. This attitude found classical expression in the work of Nahmanides, leader of the Jewish community in Barcelona in the thirteenth century.

II. Nahmanides: Compromised Medicine

According to Nahmanides, medicine is less than fully permitted, not in terms of a circumscribed scope, but rather in terms of the degree of its legitimacy. Basically incompatible with the religious ideal, medicine is no more than a tolerated practice, a compromise with human frailty:

> In general then, when Israel are in perfection and numerous, their affairs are not governed at all by the natural order of things . . .

> For God blesses their bread and their water, and removes sickness from amongst them—so that they have no need of a physician nor of observing any medical regimen. Thus was the practice of the righteous in the Prophetic Era: should they become entangled in a sin, causing them sickness, they would turn not to the physicians but to the prophets—as did Hezekiah, when he got sick (Isaiah 38). . . .

> For he who seeks God through a prophet will not consult the physicians. Indeed, what share[10] is there for physicians in the house of those who do God's will, seeing that He has assured us, "and He will bless your bread and your water, and I [=God] will remove sick-

ness from amongst you" (Exodus 23:25)—while the physicians' occupation is with nought but foods and beverages, warning against some and recommending others. . . .

Nahmanides has thus marshalled biblical support for his opposition to seeking medical help. In post-talmudic Judaism, however, direct appeal to scripture is not enough, and Nahmanides knows that he will have to come to terms with the talmudic pronouncement of a permission to heal. As a preamble to that, he adduces talmudic support for his denigration of medicine:

This is the sense of the Rabbinic comment, "Medications are not the way for people, but they have become accustomed to them" (BT *berakhot* 60a): Had they not accustomed themselves to medications, a person would have become sick in accordance with the punishment due for his sin, and would be healed at God's will. Since they, however, became accustomed to medications, God left them to the contingencies of nature.

Now the ground is laid for Nahmanides' ingenious explanation of the permission to heal. Given that the Talmud explicitly permits rendering medical treatment, how can it be supposed wrong for a patient to seek help from a physician?

This is the intent of the Rabbis' comment: "and he shall cause him to be thoroughly healed"—this implies that a physician is granted permission to heal." They did not say that the *patient* has been granted permission to be healed, but only that, once the patient has fallen ill and has come to be healed—since he had become accustomed to medications, not being of God's faithful whose share is in life—the *physician* should not refrain from healing him, whether out of concern lest he die under his hand (assuming that he is qualified in that profession), or through holding that "God alone is the Healer of all alive"—for they are thus accustomed.[11]

The perfectly righteous should know no illness. The faithful's reaction to sickness should be not a search for natural causes, but an examination of their personal behavior, seeking repentance rather than medicine.

Nahmanides's attitude regarding recourse to physicians is part of his general view about the incompatibility of true piety with reliance on natural causality.[12] He explicates this view in his commentary on a section in Deuteronomy (18:9–13) which includes a prohibition against turning to astrologers. For Nahmanides, astrology represented fully valid scientific knowledge, as he explains frankly at the outset:

[God] established that the celestial [entities] control those under them. The powers of the Earth, and everything upon it, were made to depend on the stars and constellations, following their course and attitude— as demonstrated by astrological science. (commentary to Deut. 18:9)

Why, then, were Israel enjoined not to seek guidance from experts who might validly predict the future on the basis of astral observations? The set of biblical prohibitions concludes with a demand for fidelity: "You shall be wholehearted with the Eternal your God," which Nahmanides explains thus:

[This] means that we should be inwardly dedicated to Him exclusively. We should believe that He alone does everything, and has true knowledge of all things future. From Him alone are we to enquire—through His prophets or priests[13]—regarding future events. We may not direct such enquiries to astrologers or other [diviners], nor rely on the inevitable realization of their predictions. Rather, when we learn of any

[such] prediction, we should say "All is in God's hands," for He is the God of Gods, exalted above all and completely omnipotent, who can alter at will the formations of the stars and constellations, who "frustrates the tokens of the impostors, and makes diviners mad."[14] We should believe that all coming events will be determined in accord with each person's [degree of] entering into God's service. (commentary to 18:13)

The issue is, then, one of reliance. Predictions according to the natural course of things are generally valid, but relying on them undercuts a person's total dependence on God. After all, God can override natural causality "at will"; the truly faithful should put their trust in God's direct providence, thereby retaining a "whole-hearted" existential dependence on God.

Seeking help from those who are experts in the world's natural order constitutes an inappropriate alternative—and thereby, a barrier—to pious trust in the Almighty. Turning to physicians is but one instance, albeit a common one, of such lack of trust.

As we shall see below, Maimonides took a diametrically opposite view. He did not share Nahmanides's reading of the prohibition against consulting astrologers, insisting instead that astrology was only prohibited because it is a sham, useless and potentially dangerous.[15] Conversely, he held that any sound knowledge could be employed without reservation, and strongly denounced "religious misgivings" about medicine. But in order to fully appreciate his remarks, we must say something about their context, a rabbinic discussion of the biblical King Hezekiah, and take note of rival Nahmanidean interpretations of the same discussion.

III. Hezekiah and the "Book of Healing"

King Hezekiah's deeds are described in the second books of Kings (Chapters 18–20) and Chronicles (Chapters 29–32). In some respects, he appears to exemplify perfect Nahmanidean trust. He rebels against the mighty Assyrian Empire, and in the critical hour, when all seems lost, puts his faith in God. Flying in the face of any reasonable expectation, a miraculous victory is promised by the prophet Isaiah and then comes to pass. This accords well with the prophetic demand to forgo military might in favor of relying directly on God.[16] Nahmanides, with the doctrine of "whole-hearted" trust, is a worthy heir to that prophetic stance. As we saw above, he cites Hezekiah's behavior as a model of true piety: "[the righteous] would turn not to the physicians but to the prophets—as did Hezekiah, when he got sick."

Hezekiah is, however, hardly a consistent model of exclusive dependence on God, for in other instances he shows a boldness of initiative. In fact, he did not meet the Assyrian threat with pious passivity. When removing the precious temple doors offered the only way to buy off the threatening Assyrian king, Hezekiah went ahead and ordered it done. In customary fashion, rabbinic legends embellished Hezekiah's biography with some further stories and details; the rabbis' divided view of his life is summed up in polarized scheme:

> Hezekiah, king of Judea, did six things;
> Three were endorsed [= by the sages[17]],
> and three were not endorsed.
> Three were endorsed:
> He dragged his father's bones on a bed of ropes—
>   and it was endorsed;
> He pulverized the copper snake
>   —and it was endorsed;
> And he *concealed*[18] *the Book of Healing*
>   —*and it was endorsed.*
>
> And three were not endorsed:
> He detached the temple doors and sent them to the
>   king of Assyria—and it was not endorsed; . . .

(Mishna, pesahim 4:10)

Common to the first and second items is the purpose of combatting infidelity to God. The first act took place at the beginning of Hezekiah's reign, when he carried out a religious revolution against the idolatrous practices fostered by his father Ahaz. In order to utterly denounce the dead King's deeds, his remains were subjected to flagrant indignity. The stern requirements of both royal and paternal honor were overridden by the exigencies of the political situation.[19] As to the second act, pulverizing the copper snake: although the snake was initially made by Moses himself, it had become the focus of idolatrous worship (I Kings 18:4).

Conversely, the rabbis disapprove of Hezekiah's attempt to meet a military crisis through the calculated expedient of paying tribute; he should rather have put his trust in God. That, at least, is one plausible reading, which makes fidelity to God the consistent theme of the rabbinic appraisals here, a reading fully in tune with Nahmanides's general approach. And, given Nahmanides's view of medicine, it is virtually indubitable that he understood the rabbinic praise for concealing the "Book of Healing" along similar lines, for medicine, too, constitutes a threat to pious fidelity.

We do not have explicit evidence of Nahmanides's reading of Hezekiah's deed, but we can quote here other rabbis who clearly shared his basic attitude toward medicine. For example *Rashi*, the classical commentator on the Talmud (France, eleventh century) explains that Hezekiah was reacting to the fact that the people's "heart was not humbled by illness, as they were immediately cured."[20]

A more expansive formulation of this approach is offered by *Maharsha* (Poland, sixteenth century), the most famous commentator on the *aggadic* (=non-legal) sections of the Talmud. The Talmud (*berakhot* 10b) cites Hezekiah's assertion, in praying to God, "I have done that which is good in Your eyes" (Isaiah 38:3), and in characteristic homiletical fashion seeks to spell out the specific grounds for this statement. Of all Hezekiah's meritorious deeds, it singles out the concealing of the "Book of Healing"; *Mahar-sha* explains why this deed in particular fits the Biblical phrase, "good in *Your* eyes":

> Even though, in the eyes of humans, it is not good to conceal [such a book], as they seek healing from a physician, who was indeed granted permission to heal—still in your eyes it is good, so that a person should not rely on medicine, and with humbled heart will pray for mercy.

This attitude is basically shared by commentators like R. Bahye, whose restrictive views on the permission to heal we discussed above; and as we shall presently see, it was also the target of Maimonides's polemic. Although some of its adherents antedate Nahmanides, I shall refer to their position as the "Nahmanidean view."

IV. Maimonides: Science as God's Vehicle

Maimonides, in his commentary to the Mishna in which King Hezekiah is praised for concealing the "Book of Healing," refuses to read it as endorsing a rejection of medicine. Maimonides first struggles to offer alternative accounts of Hezekiah's deed, then proceeds to strongly criticize the Nahmanidean view.

> The "Book of Healing" was some book containing manners of healing through illicit means, e.g., what the crafters of amulets imagine: that if an amulet is produced in a particular manner it will be effective regarding a certain illness—or similar forbidden things.

> Now its author composed it only as a study in the nature of reality; not aiming for any of its contents to be employed. This is permitted, as you will be taught, for things which God prohibited to practice may be studied and known—for God said (Deut. 18:9) "You shall not learn to practice," and the received interpre-

tation is "But you may learn to understand and to teach."[21] So, when people deviated and employed it for healing, he concealed it.

It is [also] possible that this was a book containing prescriptions for the preparation of poisons, e.g., "poison X is prepared thus, is administered thus, induces such and such an illness, and is cured thus and so"— so that a physician observing those symptoms shall know that poison X has been administered; he will act to neutralize it and save the patient. So, when people deviated and employed it for murder, he concealed it.

The only reason I have elaborated at length upon this matter is that I have heard, and indeed the explanation was proffered to me, that Solomon composed a Book of Healing, whereby—if a person fell ill with any illness whatsoever—he would turn to this book, follow its instructions, and be healed. Hezekiah then saw that humans were putting their trust—with respect to their illnesses—not in God, but instead in medicine; therefore he decided to conceal it.

Now, apart from this proposition's being vacuous and involving delusionary elements, its proponents attribute to Hezekiah and to his circle (who endorsed his act) a measure of foolishness that ought not to be attributed to any but the worst of the multitude. According to their defective and silly fancy, if a person is hungry and seeks bread to eat—whereby he is undoubtedly healed from that great pain—should we say that he has failed to trust in God?! "What madmen!" is the proper retort to them. For just as I, at the time of eating, thank God for having provided me with something to relieve my hunger, to sustain my life and my strength—so should I thank Him for having provided a cure which heals my illness, when I use it. There would have been no need for me to refute this inferior interpretation, were it not widespread.[22]

According to Maimonides, the notion of "forbidden medicine" can only apply to deceptive means, which are worse than useless, being the paraphernalia of idolatrous culture. The idea of a perfect cure for all ailments is, in fact, unrealistic, but prospects of enhanced human capacity to overcome illness are no threat to faith or to piety.

For Maimonides, utilization of natural causes is in no way at odds with divine works. Indeed, this is an understatement; in his view, God acts in the world chiefly or even solely through natural causality. Sound medicine, like sound technology in general, is itself an instance of God's providence; there is no alternative mode of turning directly, as it were, to divine help. So the permission to heal is no special case, no granting of a license to human agents to trespass upon a divine realm.

IV. Views of Providence and Medical Goals

This difference between Maimonides's and Nahmanides's attitudes toward natural causality implies a difference in the value-foundation of medical practice. For Nahmanides, the professed goal of medicine seems dubious at best. To the extent that, through manipulating natural causality, we can alter the patient's fate, this amounts to circumventing divine judgment. The pure religious ideal continues to beckon, inviting us to relinquish medicine in favor of repentance, falling back on God's providence. Rather than seeing himself as an agent fulfilling God's plan, the physician ought to recognize that God's plan would ideally proceed without human intervention. For if God's commandments are followed perfectly, then His providence alone will ensure the proper result.

Nahmanides's view can be a source of some embarrassment to contemporary followers of Halakha. Does he really challenge them to refrain from seeking medical help? In an effort to represent a unanimous endorsement, not only of an obligation to heal, but even of a duty to seek medical treatment, J.D. Bleich[23] seeks to harmonize the disparate views of these two medieval scholars. Nahmanides's radical position is domesticated, in Bleich's presentation, through two stratagems.

First, he demonstrates that "Nahmanides' statements, if taken literally, are contradicted by a number of Talmudic dicta." This finding is intended to support an alternate (and somewhat contrived) reading of Nahmanides's words, a conclusion which seems, however, hardly warranted. After all, Nahmanides explicitly bases his argument on other talmudic dicta; the talmudic sages might have simply disagreed among themselves on this issue, as on thousands of others.[24]

Bleich's second stratagem consists in pointing out that Nahmanides himself describes the eschewal of medicine as befitting either an ideal era or exceptional individuals. Ordinary people in ordinary times are, says Nahmanides, "left to the contingencies of nature." From this statement— an expression of unhappy resignation—Bleich concludes that they are obligated to avail themselves of the resources of medicine. This reading ignores Nahmanides's explicit insistence that the permission to combat illness through medicine had been granted, as a concession to non-ideal human frailty, only to the physician but *not* to the patient. More importantly, it severs Nahmanides's position on medicine from the roots of his religious orientation. For Nahmanides, the special commandment "You shall be whole-hearted with the Eternal your God" embodies a vital and perennial spiritual challenge.[25]

What Nahmanides offers amounts to an inverted, and thereby less problematic, version of the notorious "naturalistic fallacy" which confers normative status on an existing state of affairs.[26] In their crudest form, instances of this fallacy say something like "Since X is the way things are, it follows that X is the way things should be." Perhaps no one really subscribes to such faulty reasoning—at least not consciously.[27] Here, in any case, it is not the natural state that is deemed normative in and of itself, but rather the natural as a reflection of divine determination. Given that background belief, 'is' can here imply 'ought'; ideally, at least, God's intentions could be discerned from the actual course of events. This suggests that even if medical intervention is permitted, the physician might sometimes be able to recognize that certain of his or her efforts are opposed to God's wishes and therein be guided to stand back.

None of this is conceivable, of course, in the Maimonidean view, which encompasses medical capability itself within God's providential plan. Thus whatever is deemed desirable and appropriate constitutes the legitimate goal of medical practice; the proper outcome is not indicated by the course events would follow were it not for the medical intervention, but must be determined on some other grounds.

In the discussions that follow, we shall sometimes encounter arguments from "God's will." In the Halakhic system, this usually means the will expressed in Torah, God's revealed instruction. Since the application of Torah depends on rabbinic interpretation, the specific import of God's will with regard to any particular issue might be the subject of much debate. But apart from this (Halakhically) ordinary sense, "God's will" in Jewish bioethics is sometimes invoked in a special sense, implying that in a particular instance this will can be divined directly from the medical situation. In other statements, a given state of affairs is regarded as carrying normative force without explicit reference to divine will; still, they are often most plausibly understood as relying on a tacit assumption that God has willed the given situation.

Claims of this type appear explicitly in discussions of death and dying (see Chapter 2) and of genetic engineering. A general motto seems to be implied: "death and life ought to be left in the hands of God." But philosophical analysis shows similar claims to be implicit in a much wider array of topics, such as proposed redefinitions of parenthood (that is, the "natural/social" contrast; see Chapter 3) or the status of potential medical knowledge and consequently the force of a possible duty to acquire it (see Chapter 6).

In these various contexts, we shall closely examine arguments to the effect that God's will is evident from a patient's condition or from social/medical states of affairs. Part of our task as we proceed will be to relate any such argument to the fundamental debate on this theme between Maimonides and Nahmanides.[28]

Notes

1. In section II below, I cite Nahmanides, who adds an alternative explanation of why such permission is required.

2. Midrash Terumah, chapter 2 (reproduced in Jellinek 1853, Vol. I, pp. 107–8).

3. In his Bible commentary, Exodus 21:19.

4. Feldman (1986), "The Mandate to Heal," pp. 15–21 (citation from p. 17). Feldman may be too restrictive, however, in identifying God's authorship of illness as "rebuke or punishment." The rabbis also reflect on "chastenings of love" (BT, *berakhot* 5a); cf. Hartman (1985), pp. 195–200.

5. M. Weinberger, "Turning to Physicians According to the Halakha" (in Hebrew), in Halperin (1985), pp. 11–34. The first word of this essay's title is mistranslated in the English table of contents.

6. The contrast between humanly produced wounds and divinely induced illness is explicitly endorsed by an earlier commentator on the same verse, R. Abraham ibn Ezra (also discussed in Feldman, ibid).

7. Ibid, at 17.

8. Editor's comment, ibid. p. 18, note 28.

9. Employing the terms of Rabbinic theology, we might say that the patient was struck by God's "attribute of justice," while the physician is acting on behalf of God's "attribute of mercy." A theological discussion along these lines is developed by Feldman (1986), pp. 18–21.

10. More prosaically, this word might be translated "place"; the more literal "share" conveys the possible connotation of profit.

11. Nahmanides's commentary to the Torah, Lev. 26:11; emphasis added. Nahmanides goes on to point out that the verse being explicated defines an assailant's liability for medical expenses. The Torah "does not base its laws on miracles"; the assailant should compensate the victim on the basis of accepted practice, not ideal piety.

12. For a discussion of Nahmanides's theological positions on this and related matters, see Novak (1992).

13. Literally "His holy ones," alluding to Deut. 33:8. The author explains that his mention of priests here refers to the "Urim ve-Thumim" oracle mentioned in that verse.

14. Isaiah 44:25; Nahmanides is likely also alluding to the words that follow, "Who turns wise men backward and makes their knowledge foolish."

15. See MT, Laws concerning Idolatry 11:16, and Maimonides's "Letter on Astrology," in Twersky (1972), pp. 464–73.

16. See, e.g., Isaiah 31:1–3.

17. This refers to the sages of Hezekiah's time, whose very existence is posited by a backward projection from Rabbinic Judaism. Thus these sages' endorsements and criticisms are not part of any historical record, but rather reflect the retrospective judgments of the Rabbis.

18. The Hebrew term (ganaz) means "hide away" or bury; with regard to texts, it denotes the drastic measure of permanent removal from circulation.

19. Why, then, did the Rabbis refuse to justify the forwarding of the temple doors, which was also dictated by (military) exigency? Clearly, they did not maintain a uniform position regarding "ends versus means." Perhaps they saw a significant difference in the nature of the goals, that is, religious purging of the nation versus mundane "state reasons."

20. Rashi on pesahim 56a, s.v. ve-ganaz; in his commentary to berakhot 10b, s.v. ve-hatov, Rashi explicates Hezekiah's purpose in positive terms: he concealed the Book of Medicines "in order that they should pray for mercy."

21. See BT, sanhedrin 68a.

22. Maimonides's commentary to the mishna, *pesahim* 4:6. I thank Dr. Zvi Zohar for his meticulous examination and correction of my English version against the original Arabic.

23. "The Obligation to Heal in the Judaic Tradition: A Comparative Analysis," in Rosner & Bleich (1979), pp. 1–44.

24. Nahmanides himself emphasizes this aspect of the talmudic heritage as a major determinant of Halakhic discourse based on the Talmud. See his introduction to *milhemet hashem,* printed at the beginning of the standard (Vilna, 1881) edition of Alfasi.

25. Part of Nahmanides's critique of Maimonides's *Book of the Commandments* consists of a short alternative list of commandments which Maimonides had "failed to mention." Number 8 in this list is the commandment "to be wholehearted." For a harmonizing interpretation along similar lines, see also Weinberger (1985), pp. 21–26.

26. The precise character of the charge of "naturalistic fallacy" (originating with G.E. Moore) is an issue of some disagreement; for an argument along the lines alluded to in the text, see Hare (1952), "Description and Evaluation" (pp. 111–26).

27. Commonly, the factual observation yields its normative implication only in conjunction with normative assumptions. But these might be tacit and sometimes easily discredited when spelled out; thus people can be exposed as actually deriving 'Ought' from 'Is.'

28. Bleich's harmonization seems intended not only to blunt the Nahmanidean challenge, but also to produce the complementary suggestion that Maimonides might share a willingness to fall back, in some situations, on guidance from "God's will" in this special sense (see ibid, pp. 27–28).

2

Death: Natural Process and Human Intervention

I. The 'Active/Passive' Distinction Regarding Euthanasia

Euthanasia only becomes morally conceivable when, due to great suffering, it is against a person's interest to go on living.[1] In many situations, primarily where the person is unable to express his or her position, determining that it is best for someone to die is very complicated. But sometimes a mentally competent patient, undergoing great suffering and expecting no improvement, expresses a rational wish for release through death. In many instances, the primary moral response should be a greater commitment to pain control;[2] nevertheless, there are, and perhaps always will be, situations where there is no painless alternative. Complying with such a wish to die constitutes "voluntary euthanasia," which is the subject of the following discussion.[3]

In contemporary policy regarding euthanasia, the most crucial factor is the significance attached to the 'active/passive' distinction (killing vs. letting die).[4] In most jurisdictions, active cooperation with a patient's request to die would be criminal, while passive cooperation—such as, through foregoing certain possible treatments which the patient has either refused or simply not authorized—is normally obligatory. The distinction is similarly held to carry decisive weight in the Jewish tradition. The following statement by Isaac Klein, a prominent Conservative rabbi, is fairly representative:

> Human life is precious, and its preservation takes precedence over every other consideration. . . . [This] includes the obligation of forbearance from doing anything that might hasten the death of a sick person, no matter how serious the illness (Maimonides, Hil. Aveil 4:5). Hence, euthanasia is forbidden under any circumstance.
>
> However, if death is certain, and the patient suffers greatly, it is permissible to desist from postponing death by artificial means.[5]

This statement reflects a recognition that life can sometimes continue only at the cost of great suffering, and that from the perspective of the patient's interests, death may then be preferable. That is what justifies "desisting from postponing death"—passive euthanasia. But if a swift death is the preferred result, why may it be produced passively, which is often not the most humane way, but not actively? can a good account be offered for the distinction between the modes whereby this desired death is brought about?[6]

This has been the subject of much debate amongst moral philosophers, one which often forms along the lines of the confrontation between consequentialism and deontology. As might be expected, consequentialists tend to deny that the 'active/passive' distinction carries any moral significance; for them, it is the foreseen result that determines an action's moral character, rather than its mode of execution. A deontological perspective, however, might support the distinction, since deontology consists in judging not by the result alone, but rather by the character of the (prohibited) act; for example, the act of killing.

The basic problem for a deontological stance is how to avoid being authoritarian. "This deed is evil," but *why*, apart from its consequences, is it evil?[7] If killing is bad because it brings about another's death, then letting die is equally bad, for its result is certainly the same. Accounts of deontological judgments necessarily focus instead on the agent's perspective. This is sometimes said to involve a focus on intention; that in itself, however, is too vague, since intentions have more than one aspect. After all, killing does not differ from letting die in its intended result; if there is a difference in intention, it must derive from a difference in the nature of the (intended) act.

Judging an act to be prohibited in itself, that is, by virtue of its very description or character, involves viewing it as having a certain inherent (negative) value apart from its consequences. This seems to imply a reification of evil; the act is deemed bad in itself, prior to any judgment relating to the persons involved. The deontological approach thus shows a close affinity to religious traditions, which are frequently characterized as involving reified symbolic representations. No doubt, there are secular deontologists, but insofar as they do not rely exclusively on dogmatic pronouncements, their moral explanations will necessarily have this quasi-religious character.[8]

Let us explore the accounts offered, in the Jewish tradition, for its presumably clear opposition to voluntary active euthanasia. Through this analysis, some of the strengths as well as the limitations of a deontological approach will come to light.[9] Let us begin with a fairly representative statement of the deontological taboo against extinguishing a human life. E. Waldenberg writes: "[the patient's] consent can grant no permission to *extinguish God's candle* that is within him."[10] This image of human life as a burning candle, with the accompanying dread of touching it, harks back originally to the talmudic tractate *Semahot* (1:1–4). The teaching was codified by R. Isaac Alfasi (N. Africa, eleventh century); the gloss on Alfasi's code here, by R. Joshua Bo'az (Italy, sixteenth century), has become the classical nexus for Halakhic discussions on active/passive euthanasia. This masterpiece of reasoned casuistry turns out, upon analysis, to reflect a picture far richer and more complex than that depicted in subsequent codifications. We shall examine whether the 'candle' imagery here furnishes a coherent deontological injunction.

Admittedly, R. Bo'az's discussion makes at most a veiled allusion to the suffering involved in a protracted process of dying. His subject is not explicitly euthanasia in its precise contemporary sense of killing a (terminally ill) person in order to satisfy that person's interest in relief from suffering. Rather, he addresses the distress involved in an unusually protracted death-process. Still, relief from this process might be said to fall within the broader, literal meaning of "good death."

Let us begin with Alfasi's summary of talmudic law regarding a *gosses*, that is, a person who has entered the final phase of dying. Such a person must be treated fully and consistently as alive; things done to a newly-dead person may by no means be initiated.

II. The Flickering Candle

Alfasi (M.Q. 16b)[11]

> A *gosses* is like a live person regarding all matters. It is forbidden to tie his jaws, to stop his orifices, to place metal or cooling vessels on his navel—up to the moment he dies, as written, *"Before the silver cord is snapped asunder"* [Eccl. 12:6].[12] It is [equally] forbidden to anoint him or to wash him; to cast him upon sand or salt—until he dies. It is forbidden to close his eyes; and anyone who touches him is a shedder of blood. What is this like? Like a flickering candle; when a person touches it, it is immediately extinguished.

> *Shiltey ha-Giborim (gloss by R. Bo'az, ibid 4)*: On the basis of this, it would appear that we ought to forbid the practice of some people. When a person is *gosses*, and the soul is unable to depart, they remove the bedding from under him. For it is said that the bedding contains feathers of a certain bird which cause the soul[13] not to depart. Several times I protested vehemently, seeking to bring an end to this evil practice, but was unsuccessful. My teachers, however, disagreed with my position; and Rabbi Nathan of Hungary, of blessed memory, wrote permitting this. After several years, I found in *Sefer Hasidim* (723) support for my position. For there it is written:

> If one is *gosses* and is unable to die unless trans-
> ferred to another place, they may not move him
> away.

In truth, the pronouncements of *Sefer Hasidim* are
problematic; for he earlier wrote:

> If a man was[14] *gosses*, and adjacent to that house
> someone was chopping wood; and the soul was
> [therefore] unable to depart—they should remove
> the wood-chopper from there.

This implies the opposite of his subsequent sentence
[quoted above]! It can, however, be explained thus:
Surely, it is forbidden to do anything causing the
gosses not do die quickly, such as chopping wood
there so that the soul is hindered in its departure, or
placing salt on his tongue so that he does not die
quickly. Anything of this sort is forbidden, as clearly
implied by his language; thus in any such situation, it
is permitted to remove the [hindering] cause. But
doing something which would cause him to die
quickly, [causing] the departure of the soul—that is
forbidden. Therefore it is forbidden to transfer the
gosses from his place to another place, so that his
soul should depart; and it is also therefore forbidden
to place the synagogue keys under his pillow, for this
too hastens the departure of his soul.

From this it follows that if there is something
there which is causing his soul not to depart, it is permitted to remove that [hindering] cause. There is nothing improper in that, for [in removing it] one is not
placing one's finger on the candle, not committing any
deed. But placing anything on the *gosses*, or moving
him from one place to another so that his soul should
depart quickly—seems surely forbidden, for one is
[thereby] placing one's finger on the candle.

Here is a remarkable record of a dispute over treatment
of a dying person whose "soul is unable to depart." The

author, R. Bo'az, was strongly convinced that a practice known in his community was in violation of the talmudic norm of reverence for the dying. In his view, removing the bedding was tantamount to shedding of blood, and he "protested vehemently" to no avail. Indeed, the practice was endorsed both by his teachers and by written authority. Whatever the beliefs underlying the supposition (shared by all parties) that those feathers were efficacious in hindering the soul's departure, the practice seems morally equivalent to removal of life support. Does such removal amount to "extinguishing the flickering candle"?

R. Bo'az first thought he had found strong support in the revered twelfth century *Sefer Hasidim*,[15] but that source turned out to be more complex. Through an intricate analysis of various cases and rulings, R. Bo'az works his way to a principled distinction. Although in the final paragraph the permission seems to hinge on whether one is "committing any deed," the significant contrast seems crucially different from the familiar distinction between active and passive measures.

Our text presents a knotty question of interpretation: did R. Bo'az finally come to accept the practice which he had at first considered tantamount to murder? There is some ambiguity due to the fact that the initial condemnation is never explicitly retracted. It seems to me, however, that the whole point of the last paragraph lies in coming to terms with this reversal. Indeed, the author's intellectual struggle seems to consist precisely in the effort to distinguish an action, such as removing the bedding, from the forbidden "placing of one's finger on the candle."[16] The bedding initially seemed part and parcel of the normal setting; its removal thus appeared to be a sinful intrusion into the course of events. But finally, the normative frame of reference is narrowed to processes within the patient's immediate person, and effects on these processes by any objects or activities, even those in close proximity, are deemed external.

III. A Version of Deontology:
Respecting 'Natural' Death

The prevalent picture of a common attitude in Jewish bioethics, as reflected in the quote from Klein at the head of this chapter, was of an active/passive distinction. However, our analysis of central traditional sources has revealed a principle not of passivity, but rather of respecting and facilitating—whether passively or actively—a natural death process.

True, neither the term "natural," nor any equivalent term, is employed explicitly, but something like it appears necessary for making sense of the argument. The basic norm is put in terms of causal intervention. Hastening or hindering the death process must *both equally* be not only (passively) avoided but also (actively) prevented. This position crucially depends on presuming an autonomous pace of the death process. Given that presumption, the talmudic emphasis on "not touching the flickering candle" is understood in terms of non-interference; the dying of a *gosses* must be allowed to proceed at its own pace.

While it is considered wrong to allow the persistence of a hindrance to this process, failure to remove such a hindrance is, it seems, not as severe as the opposite sin of hastening death, which constitutes "bloodshed." Still, the hindrance should be removed, letting the *gosses* die earlier. This clearly excludes an understanding of the forbidden hastening of death in consequentialist terms: the deed's wrongness is not determined by its result (namely, the fact that the patient is dead at a certain earlier moment) but rather by its symbolic characterization as "extinguishing the candle." Reified evil is the netherside of reified good, for the negative value of 'extinguishing' derives from the positive value of the 'candle', that is, from the sanctity ascribed to human life. We have thus come up with a *naturalistic deontology*: what must be respected is the natural expiration of human life in its own due course.

A proper explication of this view requires at least two steps. Ultimately there must be some account of *why* the natural process ought to be respected, but first it must be possible to reliably determine just what is natural. In R. Boʻazʼs conclusion, our deep reverence is directed toward the life of the patient (and its ending in death) in isolation from his or her environment, stripped of the artificial effects of external substances, materials, and sense stimuli.

Which effects are, then, to be deemed artificial? Moving the patient "from one place to another so that his soul should depart quickly" is forbidden;[17] this would constitute "hastening" his death. But why is the new location thought to offer a hastening of death, rather than the old location hindering it? Somehow the present room, unlike the bedding or the intruding noise, is considered part of the natural setting. Presumably, the same would apply to food and drink (although perhaps a *gosses* is unable to eat). Where—and on what grounds—should the line be drawn?

This brings to mind the problems involved in attempts to distinguish, in the modern context, between "ordinary" and "extraordinary" means of sustaining life. Yet for understanding the medieval traditions, it seems essential to emphasize their background of limited medical capability. All these rulings apply only to persons in the condition of *gosses*, a category which evidently was clearly identifiable.

To get a sense of this category, we may refer to R. Joseph Caroʼs sixteenth century code, the *Shulhan ʻArukh*. The "laws concerning a *gosses*" begin with the prohibitions regarding hastening the death of a *gosses*; the following section reads: "A person who is told ʻit is now three days since we saw your relative gossesʼ should observe the rituals of mourning, for that relative has surely died" (YD 339:2). Clearly, a gosses is conceived as a patient who will not live more than three days; he is already dying, and the issue is only just how fast (or how slow) the process will be.

This understanding poses a difficult problem for modern application of the medieval "hands-off" norm of respect for the process of dying. The notion of *gosses* reflects recognition of an inexorable final-stage process of dying. In the contemporary setting of intensive care, however, a person can be kept dying much longer than three days, sometimes almost indefinitely. This setting has made it much more difficult to discern 'natural' limits. Has contemporary medicine rendered obsolete the norm of respect for natural dying?

Here it becomes necessary to move beyond the conceptual problem of defining what is "natural"; we must delve more deeply into the question of the plausibility of naturalism, that is, of referring to "the natural" as a normative guide. Hence our analysis proceeds to step two: why should the natural process be respected?

Recalling the Maimonidean approach to medicine and nature as described in the previous chapter, all the above distinctions seem hardly comprehensible. Suppose we accept Maimonides's assertion that there is no substantial difference between the naturalness of food and that of medications. Why should any form of intervention, employing salt, sound, or whatever, not be considered part of the 'natural' factors which determine the time of death? On what basis might their presence be judged a hindrance, rather than their removal an illicit hastening?

The stance of non-intervention is compatible, it seems, only with the alternative approach to medicine advocated (above) by Nahmanides; in principle, it is not for human agents to interfere in God's providential steering of events. Medicine, which constitutes an attempt to rely on human wisdom instead of seeking God's goodwill, may be practiced "under a cloud," as it were, only by way of a compromise with impiety. But the physician's license to intervene might be suspended at the approach of death; once it becomes clear that human attempts are failing, no interference in the dying process is permitted. The natural pace of death is directed by God and must be respected by human agents.

IV. Naturalism, Providence, and Modern Medicine

How might this naturalistic doctrine be applied in the context of contemporary medical practice? In concrete terms, the issue is how to define the category of *gosses*. Suppose the rule about mourning mentioned above is turned into a formal definition: a *gosses* is a person who will certainly not survive more than three days. Then a crucial question arises: 'survive'—with or without life support?[18]

Historically, the *gosses* was surely expected to die within three days despite any medical efforts. In formal parallel, it might be suggested that the status of *gosses* today should apply only to a patient who cannot survive for three days even on life support. The category would, on this interpretation, have become virtually obsolete. But it would be strange if this were taken to imply that nowadays very few people reach a final phase of dying! Would Nahmanideans grant that God had conceded to modern physicians His control of dying?

The Nahmanidean perspective seems instead to require the opposite interpretation. Since the point is to acknowledge the limits of human intervention, life-support must be excluded from the prognosis. Most patients who would have been considered *gosses* four hundred years ago should be similarly classified today; these are persons for whom, without medical intervention, death is imminent. A position along these lines has been formulated by H.D. ha-Levi, current chief Rabbi of Tel-Aviv, who cites the "grain of salt" precedent as a model for contemporary illicit hindrance of the death ordained by God:

> . . . the permission to remove a grain of salt is undisputed and clear . . . Now a respirator is exactly the same. For this patient, upon being delivered to the hospital in a critical condition, was immediately attached to the respirator and was revived with *artificial life* in order to try and treat him and to cure him. So when the physicians come to the conclusion that there is no cure for his condition, it is clearly permitted to disconnect the patient from the machine to which he was attached.

. . . Indeed it seems to me that even if the physicians should wish to persist in keeping him alive by means of a respirator, they are not permitted to do so . . . Not only is there permission to disconnect him from the respirator, but there is a duty to do so. Since surely the person's soul, which is God's property, has already been withdrawn by God from this person, as upon removal of the machine he will immediately die.[19]

In comparison with contemporary practice and expectations, this surely implies far too much. True, a crucial pitfall is avoided by requiring first that there be no prospects of "a cure for his condition." After all, many persons who are severely ill or wounded would die but for medical intervention, and "permission has been granted to heal." It would be absurd to disallow such intervention on the grounds that the patient is "inevitably dying," based on the observation that he cannot (now) survive unaided for three days.[20] Ha-Levi explicitly condones sustaining a patient in "artificial" life as a *temporary* measure, with a view to the return of "natural" life, that is, the capability for living without life-supporting accessories.[21] But if complete recovery is indeed never expected, Ha-Levi's logic seems to prohibit sustaining a person in artificial life. The specific case under discussion is apparently one of a patient in coma, but the author's argument as stated would apply equally to an ambulatory patient supported by a mobile ventilator; upon its removal he would immediately die. Is such a person's life also to be considered artificial, and therefore not to be sustained?

The difficulty does not seem to lie merely in Ha-Levi's radical formulation of the argument; rather, it appears to be inherent in employing the Nahmanidean approach for guidance in dilemmas of contemporary end-stage medicine. If an irreversible critical condition is to indicate the limit of divine permission, then surely the condition's onset must be determined by reference to the patient's natural condition, stripped of respirator, intravenous hydration, and perhaps even aided feeding. Neither Ha-Levi nor any contemporary halakhic writer seems prepared to accept such a sweeping disavowal of human intervention at the end of life.

It may, nevertheless, be possible to formulate a more refined Nahmanidean position, although as far as I know, such a refinement has yet to be offered. This would involve redefining the *gosses* category so as to designate—against the backdrop of contemporary medicine—a final stage of the dying process. It would be interesting to see such a position worked out in detail; this would have to include, of course, convincing modes of distinguishing the natural process itself from illicit interference.

The alternative consists in reverting to the Maimonidean position, which had excluded "limitations by providence" all along. This amounts to a practical abandonment of the *gosses* category.[22] Our enhanced capabilities in keeping people alive preclude falling back on "respect for a natural process" for guidance regarding when to desist. Responsibility has shifted decisively into human hands, and substantive moral guidelines must be fashioned independently.

It might be argued that the medieval recognition and respect for "natural dying" has been recaptured and continued in the Hospice Movement. But even this continuation involves a significant transformation, as opting for a hospice reflects a conscious, responsible decision to forgo available procedures, based on a moral judgment that this way is better.

It must moreover be emphasized that hospices offer no more than a limited adherence to naturalism, set within the larger context of pervasive medical interventionism. People arrive at the hospice in a more or less terminal condition, with a medical/personal history shaped by the capabilities and accepted procedures of modern medical technology. Even if further intervention is mostly avoided, the course of their ensuing fate is hardly natural in any pure sense. Insofar as the deontological ethos of respect for the "Flickering Candle" is grounded in naturalism (or in its religious, Nahmanidean counterpart), it seems deeply incompatible with contemporary medicine. But can there be no other account of a deontological prohibition against hastening death?

V. God as Owner

The image of the dying person as "candle" is expounded by E. Waldenberg, a prominent scholar and member of the rabbinic court in Jerusalem, in another way which seems logically independent of naturalism with its attendant problems:

> "And although we see him suffering greatly in dying so that death is good for him, nevertheless we are forbidden to do anything to hasten his death, as the universe and all within it belongs to the Holy One, Blessed be He, and such is His Exalted will." . . .[23]

> No creature in the world owns a person's soul; this includes also that person himself, who has no license at all regarding his own soul nor is it his property. Thus his granting license can be of no avail concerning something which does not belong to him, but rather it is the property of God, Who alone bestows it and takes it away.

The first passage (a quotation from the nineteenth century codifier, Rabbi Y. Epstein) is indeed remarkable in its candid admission that it is truly in this person's interest to die promptly: "death is good for him." This is not the all-too-familiar argument that any wish to die is irrational, a merely subjective desire contrary to the patient's objective interests.[24] We are told, however, that the candle is "God's candle," and His proprietary interest must prevail over against the interests and wishes of the suffering patient.

But Waldenberg's position is subtly different from that expressed in the source he is expounding. R. Epstein had emphasized God's universal sovereignty: ". . . the universe and all within it belongs to the Holy One, Blessed be He."

This was meant to provide the basis for the demand to bow to the divine will. Waldenberg is much more specific; of all God's possessions, human life is singled out as that whose destruction amounts to usurpation of the divine title. This focusing-in seems designed to meet the difficulty discussed above regarding theistic naturalism, namely the question, how are we to know the proper limits for human intervention in God's world? The proposed answer lies in giving the notion of God as "owner" the specific import that He alone may induce death.

Singling out death as God's special domain may seem arbitrary; moreover, it would bespeak a grim theology in which God is posited as the exclusive producer of death alone. In fact, Waldenberg's point is rather different, more along the lines expressed in Jewish liturgy, where God is exalted as "King who brings life *and* death." The last sentence of the above quote expressly indicates such a two-sided recognition of God's power over life. He both "bestows it *and* takes it away."

Waldenberg's point in this conjunction is, of course, to provide an argument that women and men cannot produce human life without God's help, and therefore may not act on their own to destroy it. But once this wider perspective is adopted, we again face the basic inconsistency of religious naturalism, for with regard to bestowing life, God acts through human agency (some of the problems relating to human control of procreation will be examined in the next chapter). Why should the same not hold for ending life?[25]

It is worth examining a central talmudic proof-text adduced by Waldenberg in support of his demand that we reserve for God alone the taking of human life. I shall argue that, in producing a partial and out-of-context quotation, Waldenberg squanders the richness of his talmudic source, with its keen awareness of the complexities of religious naturalism and human intervention.

The talmudic passage is set in the context of Roman persecutions in second century Judea; it tells the story of Rabbi Hanina ben Teradion's martyrdom by fire. When his disciples suggested that he hasten his soul's departure by inhaling the flames, he refused, proclaiming that "it is better that it be taken by Him who has bestowed it." Here, argues Waldenberg, the implications of God's ownership are spelled out clearly. The proper norm is set by this courageous lesson, taught by R. Hanina in the face of great suffering and imminent death. Now let us look at the story in full:

> When R. Yose ben Kisma fell ill, R. Hanina ben Teradion went to visit him. R. Yose said, "Hanina, my brother, do you not know that this [Roman] nation was given reign from heaven? For it has destroyed God's house, burned His Temple Hall, killed His pious ones, and exterminated His best ones, and yet endures! I hear, however, that you sit engaged in Torah [study], and call public assemblies with a Torah scroll held in your bosom." He answered: "From Heaven they will have mercy." Said [R. Yose]: "I speak to you words of reason, and you reply, 'From Heaven they will have mercy'! I will be surprised if they don't burn you along with the Torah scroll." . . .

> Soon afterward, R. Yose ben Kisma passed away. All the Roman notables came to his funeral, and made a great eulogy. On their way back, they saw R. Hanina ben Teradion sitting engaged in Torah [study], [having] called a public assembly with a Torah scroll held in his bosom. They brought him in and wrapped him in the Torah scroll, surrounded him with bundles of vine shoots, and set them on fire. They brought tufts of wool, soaked them in water, and placed them over his heart, so that his soul should not depart quickly. . . .

> His disciples said to him, "Open your mouth, so that the fire will enter you quickly!" R. Hanina replied: "It is better that it be taken by Him who has bestowed it—a person should not harm himself!"

> The executioner said to him: "Master, if I increase the flames and remove the tufts of wool from over your

heart, will you bring me into the life of the world-to-come?" "Yes." "Swear to me!"—R. Hanina swore to him. The executioner then increased the flames and removed the tufts of wool from over his heart, and R. Hanina's soul departed quickly. The executioner forthwith threw himself into the fire; a divine voice announced: "R. Hanina ben Teradion and his executioner are assigned to life in the world-to-come." (BT *'avoda zara* 18a)

The preamble presents a fascinating argument about what it means to live in accord with heavenly guidance. R. Yose is prepared to infer divine will from the course of history; Rome's success against God's people and temple shows that it has been appointed "from heaven." It is thus God's will that His own commandments, even the supremely valued study of Torah, be abandoned in obedience to this appointed reign. R. Hanina, however, is unwilling to accord normative status to historical events. Roman power rather signals, for him, a challenge which should be met with courage and with hope that "from heaven" there will come miraculous support for those adhering to God's Torah.

R. Hanina's position resembles that of Nahmanides: piety involves eschewing pragmatic, reasonable predictions and relying instead on God's direct providence. Yet R. Yose, too, seems to be preaching a similar ethic of submitting to God's will (which he, however, takes to demand obedience to Rome). A truly Maimonidean position here would call for incorporating possibilities of human intervention within the scope of God's will. If the Jews could successfully revolt, then the choice between submission and martyrdom would not exhaust their religiously valid options.[26] If, however, a revolt is deemed futile, then a pragmatic accommodation to the Roman decrees might be the proper form of human reaction to that historical situation.

The heart of the story tells of R. Hanina's martyrdom. It is here that Waldenberg, like several other Halakhic writers, finds a paradigm for the predicament of the suffering, terminal patient. Although the cause of his troubles was not illness, R. Hanina was facing imminent death, and by hastening it he could escape protracted suffering. When his disciples suggest that he do just that, he rejects their proposal, and his answer is taken as the proper theological response: God alone, who gave life, has the prerogative of taking it.

This is true as far as it goes. R. Hanina's language does not necessarily translate into an idiom of ownership,[27] but the recognition of God as one's creator, expressed in a pious readiness to suffer unto death, may indeed inspire a similar attitude in the context of terminal illness, excluding both suicide and euthanasia. This is, however, only one part of the story. Reading on, we are forced to ask: why does R. Hanina accept the executioner's offer, rather than persevere in waiting for God to take his soul? After all, the executioner's subsequent deeds amount to both passive and active euthanasia. While removing the tufts of wool could conceivably be explained as allowing 'natural' death to occur, is not the more compassionate increasing of the flames (followed by the executioner's own suicide!) equally endorsed by the talmudic storyteller and by the heavenly voice?

Little would be gained, of course, by focusing instead only on the story's end, suppressing R. Hanina's pious steadfastness. It also seems hard to produce a satisfactory resolution of the internal tension, or any simple explanation for R. Hanina's apparent inconsistency. My point is rather that the talmudic tale, in its very complexity, does more justice to the anguish of this kind of human situation than any one-dimensional simplification. R. Hanina proclaims God as the source of life, but what this proclamation finally implies seems far from clear. Put in Waldenberg's terms of "ownership," the question is: must we necessarily assume that God insists on such total control of His human subjects?

Admittedly, contemplating the contradictory implications of a profound story is hardly a recipe for defining specific norms. Perhaps Waldenberg, then, seeking to produce an authoritative statement, considered himself bidden to resolve the tension of the talmudic tale.[28] But if so, why give absolute priority to R. Hanina's initial reluctance? Turning to Halakhic teachings regarding suicide, we find the disciples' plea to avert torture by hastening death clearly reflected in mainstream sources.

VI. Suicide and Suffering: The Case of King Saul

The Halakhic-theistic argument against voluntary euthanasia refers back to the prohibition on suicide, employing a notion of God's "ownership" which is, I think, best understood in terms of sovereignty. Accordingly, the Rabbis expressed the prohibition on suicide in terms of a post-mortem hearing before a heavenly court and proclaimed that God would hold an individual accountable for taking his own life (Gen. Rab. 34:13).

But while divine sovereignty may imply moral *accountability* for an act of suicide, it does not imply that the act is always *wrong*. Indeed, the same rabbinic source also pronounces two exceptions. These are not described in substantive form but are rather defined by pointing to Biblical examples. The two instances of legitimate suicide are those of

1. Saul (I Sam. 31: 1–6; cf. also II Sam. 1: 1–16), and
2. Hananiah, Mishael and 'Azariah (Dan. ch. 3; cf. ibid 1:7).

The second of these involves martyrdom: the three Jewish youngsters were prepared to be thrown into the furnace rather than worship an idol. The teaching that death should be chosen over idolatry, whether by submitting to the sword of oppressors or by actively killing oneself to avoid forced conversion, is pervasive in rabbinic and medieval sources and is wholly consistent with the assertion of God's sovereignty over life and death. A martyr, choosing death, is doing anything but pitting his own interests against those of God.

In the first exception, that of Saul, however, there is no evidence for a divine interest being served by the self-inflicted death. The primary biblical account reads:

The battle raged around Saul, and some of the archers hit him, and he was severely wounded[29] by the archers. Saul said to his arms-bearer, "Draw your sword and run me through, so that the uncircumcised may not run me through and make sport of me."

But his arms-bearer, in his great awe, refused; whereupon Saul grasped the sword and fell upon it.

Saul knew that he was doomed; fearing torture (and perhaps also degradation), he took his own life, and the Rabbis made his deed a paradigm of legitimate suicide. Saul's death has been the focus of much discussion in the subsequent Halakhic tradition, from the Middle Ages down to the present,[30] and three basic approaches can be discerned.[31] One approach assimilates Saul's self-inflicted death to the model of martyrdom; Saul was afraid of being tortured not only because of the physical suffering, but also—and crucially—because he would be driven to apostasy.[32] Historically, this interpretation seems rooted more in the harsh and heroic epoch of Jewish communities under the Crusades than in the biblical account itself. Applied to the context of illness, this might suggest a legitimation of suicide where a person feared that his or her suffering might lead to blasphemy.

A second approach reads the Midrashic statement about Saul not as justifying but merely as excusing. On this view, Saul's fear was indeed of physical suffering; being thus impelled by powerful emotion, he is not held liable for killing himself. Here, too, the statement about Saul is assimilated to a well-known model. Since culpable suicide entailed in principle certain social and ritual sanctions, the issue of the deceased's emotional incapacity has long been raised as a compelling excuse.[33] Thus a person facing a tortured death is never *permitted* to take his own life; insofar as he is able to abide by the proper norm, he may not commit suicide. But once he has in fact killed himself, we are to adopt the sympathetic presumption of non-liability due to compulsion.

This view has had several adherents and is the one adopted by Waldenberg in another paragraph of the same essay. Its hermeneutic weakness lies in the disanalogy with the other exception in the main source (Gen. Rab.) cited above. After all, those who give up their lives as martyrs are not merely excused but rather justified—indeed, highly praised—for their deed. But it seems that the proponents of this approach, like those of the first one, are prepared to accept hermeneutic difficulties so that Saul's death should not read as a justified suicide to avert a painful death.

A third approach, however, adopts just such a reading, focusing on the explicit circumstances of Saul's death in the biblical account. Rather than introducing conditions unique to the doomed king, Nahmanides writes simply:

> And likewise [inculpable is] an adult who kills himself because of a menace, like King Saul, who killed himself; indeed this was permitted to him. For thus we read in Genesis Rabbah: ". . . Could this apply to one who is trapped like Saul?" . . .

Nahmanides, whose position became the mainstream Halakhic ruling,[34] certainly does not deny God's sovereignty; nor does he doubt that suicide is in general wrong. But accepting God as sovereign does not imply that He is a master without compassion. Why must we assume that He insists on His "owner's rights" through untold suffering and to the bitter end? How indeed can we know that "such is His Exalted Will"?

God's will, insofar as it is reflected in Halakhic teachings, is here surely ambiguous, for the tradition presents several alternative views of a crucial exception to the prohibition on suicide. Despite this, Waldenberg writes:

> There is *not any basis for permission* nor any license for physicians to decide on modes of death-treatment for a patient, whatever the state of his suffering, and whatever their conclusion regarding the impossibility

of his recovery or of improvement in his condition. And if they—spare us!—dare do so, even if they *don a cloak of pity* and of compassionate action in shortening the suffering of the dying, nevertheless they are considered full murderers and their verdict is sealed in the Halakhic literature of our holy Torah. (ibid, emphasis added)

In light of what we have seen of the tradition, this stark denial can only mean there is not any *valid* basis for permission. Waldenberg is adopting a sharp polemical stance which leads him even to denying the moral sincerity of the rival position. Other Halakhic writers, however, have been quite prepared to draw an analogy from the King Saul tradition to the context of illness. Rabbi R.A. ben-Shim'on (chief Rabbi of Cairo, 1891–1921) tells of a terminally ill woman in his community who was suffering great pain:

At one point, driven by the fierce and overbearing pain she was suffering (may God spare us), and knowing that she had no hope of a cure, she threw herself out of the window, her death following quickly. I issued instructions to the effect that she should in no way be treated as a suicide.

The author proceeds to justify his ruling by reference to an early nineteenth century Halakhic commentator, Zvi Hirsh b. 'Azriel. Based on the mainstream tradition with regard to King Saul, R. Zvi Hirsh permits suicide to a Jew facing torture in the hands of "gentile courts."[35] From this, Ben-Shim'on argues regarding the woman who had been suffering in her terminal illness:

This follows by way of *a fortiori* reasoning from the statement of *Bet Lehem Yehuda*, that if one kills himself out of fear lest he fall into the hands of the gentile courts, and be subjected to severe tortures—this is not to be considered suicide [even if, unlike Saul, that person is not certain of imminent death]. . . .[36]

Now, that refers only to a fear of things yet to come, namely, lest they torture him; it is, moreover, uncertain. Besides, when he kills himself he is still healthy and in one piece, fearing but future suffering. How much more so then in the case before us, where she is suffering and oppressed by severe and bitter pains, and is dead while yet alive (may God spare us); she is already like a dead person.[37] (Ben Shim'on 1908, section 47)

We are faced with two disparate theological positions. For some Halakhic writers, an act aimed toward escaping suffering through death constitutes a Promethean revolt against divine rule. For others, it is plain that God would not stake His claim to mastery of the universe on the prolonged suffering of a human being at death's door.[38] God's greatness could rather be reflected in depth of compassion, allowing suicide which shortens terminal suffering.

We can, then, conclude with confidence that condemnation of such suicide is hardly the only voice in the Halakhic tradition; nor is such condemnation entailed by the tradition's basic values. Suicide is in general forbidden, but a mainstream position defines a highly relevant exception. Therefore the staple argument, "Since suicide is forbidden, voluntary euthanasia is certainly never permitted," must fail. But then, where a patient is unable to kill herself unaided, does it follow that others may or even should help her achieve the same result?

VII. Helping Another to Die

Can it make sense to say, "You could legitimately commit suicide, but it would be wrong for me to assist you"? In legal terms, this is indeed the situation today in many jurisdictions: suicide itself has been decriminalized, while assisting in suicide remains a criminal offense. But this legal difference is wholly consistent with moral condemnation of suicide itself, for not every immoral act is or should be a crime.

The moral issue is, however, very different for those who hold that, under certain circumstances, suicide is not just legally tolerated but also morally condoned. Can it then be wrong to assist a person who, lacking the physical capacity to commit suicide, expresses a competent request for help? Moreover, the morality of extending such help need not be circumscribed by the legal line which separates assisted suicide from active euthanasia. If the deed is good, perhaps it is equally good to support it, whether indirectly or directly!

Several Halakhic writers, however, explicitly maintain the prohibition of direct killing by another hand, even while endorsing the permission for suicide. P. Toledano[39] (1986), for example, offers an extensive analysis and concludes that, following the main line of Halakhic tradition, the Saul precedent permits suicide to escape suffering at death's door. Yet he goes on to write that "*Actively killing* a suffering patient is completely forbidden and constitutes murder" (emphasis added). This language suggests a condoning of aid which does not involve "actively killing." Apparently, Toledano's permission includes both suicide and assisting in suicide; these are contrasted with active euthanasia, which "constitutes murder."

Indeed, condoning suicide itself seems to entail endorsement of assistance therein. If choosing death is morally and theologically justified for the patient, then how can it be wrong to lend assistance in this where necessary? It seems clear that our moral judgment of a deed defined as "assisting in . . . X" must depend on the moral quality attached to the primary deed X. It seems to follow, furthermore, that extending such aid is not only permitted, but even morally required. Insofar as one agrees that a particular situation justifies a deed, one is bound to help it be accomplished.

Things become more difficult, of course, if the person being asked to assist does not share the patient's view of the matter. This may be either because they differ in assessing the situation ("No, you are wrong; going on living like that is not worse than death") or because they take different moral positions. In the present context, we shall focus on the second kind of disagreement.

Suppose, then, that the patient adheres to what I have termed the "mainstream view" and considers his situation analogous to that of King Saul. Accordingly, he intends to commit suicide and asks someone else for necessary assistance. This other person, however, subscribes (let's suppose) to Waldenberg's view that no degree of suffering can justify suicide: it is always a usurpation of God's right. Should she act against her own convictions?

The Halakhic tradition is imbued with principled disagreements, and in ancient times it came to formulate a simultaneous acceptance of mutually contrary teachings. Of the classical disputes between the Houses of Shammai and Hillel it is said, "these and those are the words of the living God."[40] Faced with rival interpretations of the Saul precedent, a similar acceptance seems indicated. Perhaps, then, she can say, "I believe you are wrong to do this, but I respect your decision and out of compassion will help you implement it."

In any case, Toledano would apparently allow one to assist in a suicide that one considers justified by the circumstances. Yet even given such circumstances, he strictly forbids active euthanasia. Even the patient's own request to die cannot, he explains, remove the prohibition of killing him, because "his body is not his property, to be destroyed at will"; the owner is God. But if God's ownership precludes human intervention to shorten terminal suffering, why is suicide itself permitted?

The inconsistency arises not so much from Toledano's particular reason as from the very structure of the position he espouses. The same problem applies regardless of the particular grounds for forbidding suicide, whether they are "ownership," respect for a "natural" process of dying, or whatever. Once the prohibition is qualified to allow suicide in certain circumstances, it is difficult to support an unqualified prohibition of active euthanasia in similar circumstances where the patient is simply unable to effect his or her own death.

This difficulty can only be overcome by showing a qualitative distinction between a deed of suicide and one of killing. Now, the rabbis' hermeneutic does not derive the suicide prohibition from the same verse that prohibits murder,[41] and thus leaves formal room for such a distinction. But formal possibility is not enough; we would need a substantive account of how these are two distinct evils.

Neither religious naturalism nor the doctrine of divine ownership seems capable of furnishing such an account, although (separately or combined) they can support a deontological prohibition of taking human life. As we saw, this prohibition need not be deemed absolute, as it might not extend to conditions of terminal suffering. Nevertheless, some authors do endorse such an absolute version, and their view, although not (as we have seen) without its difficulties, is certainly coherent. It does not, however, leave room for a halfway house. If it is acceptable to God that a terminally suffering person should "extinguish the candle" by his or her own hand, why should not the same apply to the hand of another?

From a Maimonidean perspective, the entire concern here over encroaching on God's realm is, of course, misconceived. It is the responsibility of human agents to work toward any worthy end; thus it certainly appears that others ought to do whatever is necessary to help the suffering patient. If the Saul precedent is accepted in its mainstream version, there is no justification for a deontological prohibition of voluntary active euthanasia. This does not, however, automatically imply the actual endorsement of such a practice. It might still be maintained that active euthanasia differs from assisting in suicide because of its dangerous broader consequences.

This brings us to the "slippery slope" argument, which is indeed also adduced by Waldenberg (albeit as an ancillary one). Classically it begins by conceding, at least for the sake of argument, that active euthanasia may in itself sometimes be justified. It goes on to claim that such euthanasia must, nevertheless, always be disallowed in order to avoid dire consequences. Once voluntary euthanasia is permitted, the argument runs, we shall unavoidably go downhill to allowing quasi-voluntary and finally even involuntary euthanasia, with "presumed consent" and similar notions playing their evil part.

These are serious concerns, and they should not be lightly dismissed. The issue is basically factual and should be judged, insofar as possible, on the basis of empirical investigations.[42] In any case, shifting the basis for the prohibition onto these grounds signifies the crossing of a crucial divide in our normative discourse. For the issue now is one of balancing the prospect of helping an individual out of his or her misery against the need to protect others from expected harm. Even on the mainstream reading of the Saul precedent, the compassionate duty may sometimes have to give way to considerations of responsible policy. This is, however, very different from the common assertion that (in Jewish bioethics) active euthanasia is inherently and absolutely objectionable.

Notes

1. Sometimes euthanasia is proposed for an unconscious patient, e.g., one in PVS (=permanent vegetative state); arguably, the situation involves no suffering, yet it would be right to (say) discontinue ventilation. One line of justifying this holds that in entering PVS a person ceases to exist; in that case, discontinuing ventilation is not killing. The issue is one of euthanasia only if such a patient is deemed, instead, still alive. But then the interests of this person ought to prevail, and killing him or her must be justified (if it can be justified) in terms of these interests. In other words, it would have to be argued that, despite being unconscious, it is not good for this person to go on living in PVS.

2. See, e.g., Twycross (1981).

3. If voluntary euthanasia is judged acceptable, then the further issues involved in non-voluntary euthanasia need to be addressed, such as advance directives, proxy, or surrogate decision making, etc. The discussion here focuses, however, on the fundamental problem of voluntary euthanasia.

4. The ongoing philosophical discussion on this issue is well-anthologized in Steinbock and Norcross (1994); see especially the last chapter there, Jeff McMahan's, "Killing, Letting Die, and Withdrawing Aid," pp. 383–420.

5. Klein (1979), 272–73; references are given to the Talmud ('avoda zara 18a and ketubot 104a); to Shulhan 'Arukh (Y.D. 339:1 in Rema—see n. 16 below); and to F. Rosner's discussion, "Jewish Attitude Toward Euthanasia" [in his Modern Medicine and Jewish Law, N.Y., 1972]. In numerous contemporary representations of the Jewish tradition, this distinction is likewise held to be greatly significant. This view is expressed, inter alia, in Herring (1984), ch. 3, "Euthanasia," pp. 67–90; and by I. Jakobovits, "Ethical Problems Regarding the Termination of Life," in Meier (1986), pp. 84–95, at 90. In their perception of the tradition, Reform scholars have reflected a similar position, although some of them also express moral disagreement with it. See the various statements in the Central Conference of American Rabbis Yearbook, vol. 58 (1950), 107–20.

6. The major imperative for confronting this problem is that sometimes passive euthanasia is far crueler. See, e.g., J. Rachels, "Active and Passive Euthanasia" (1975), reprinted in Steinbock & Norcross (1994), pp. 112–19.

7. The difficulties involved in giving a rational account of non-consequentialist prohibitions are canvassed by S. Scheffler (1982), pp. 80–129.

8. Compare the discussion in Dworkin (1993), ch. 3: "What is Sacred?" pp. 68–101. Dworkin's argument regarding the affinity between secular and religious valuations is, I think, quite powerful, even if the constitutional implications he draws from this are dubious.

9. In this context, listening to voices of specific traditions (based on the pluralistic approach defined in the Introduction) seems the only meaningful way to proceed. Clearly, a discussion of some abstract "deontological approach" is even more transparently difficult than addressing an unspecific "consequentialism."

10. R. E. Waldenberg, from section 29 of the tractate "Ramat Rachel," published in 1965 in vol. 8 of his responsa, Tsits Eliezer (emphasis added). More of this tractate will be quoted and discussed below.

11. Unlike Maimonides, who a century later codified talmudic law in an entirely new scheme, according to subjects Alfasi's code follows the talmudic arrangement of material. Alfasi's work is thus better described as a Halakhic abridgement of the Talmud. The reference here is thus to tractate *mo'ed qatan*, although Alfasi is quoting from the talmudic "Tractate of Mourning" (*Semahot*); the citation refers to the separate Alfasi pagination. For an English translation of the source, see *The Minor Tractates, semahoth*, tr. A. Cohen, London: Soncino (second edition, 1971) pp. 326–27.

12. The allusion is to a section in Ecclesiastes (12:1–7) describing the end of life.

13. The text here reads *nefesh*, while the initial reference (also translated as "soul") was to *neshama*; they are used here, it seems, interchangeably.

14. I have retained the original's shift from past tense here to 'should' below; this seems to reflect the source of this ruling, in an actual case: "A man was *gosses*," etc.

15. The book is attributed to Rabbi Judah the Pious, the central figure of the Pietistic movement in Ashkenaz (=Germany).

16. A contrary reading was adopted by *Rema* (=Rabbi M. Isserless), author of the influential glosses to *Shulhan 'Arukh.* His gloss to Y.D. 339:1, which clearly derives from R. Bo'az's discussion and reaffirms his basic "non-intervention" principle, omits any mention of opposing views (e.g., that of Rabbi Nathan). Later commentators labored to resolve the prohibition on removing the bedding, which was thus retained, with the permission to remove the grain of salt. An English rendition of *Rema*'s gloss is given in Sinclair (1989), pp. 11–12.

For an illuminating survey of contemporary interpretations and implementations of these and other sources, see Newman (1990).

17. Even, according to the source in *Sefer Hasidim*, at the patient's express request.

18. For the same question regarding the definition of "terminal," cf. Meisel (1995), vol. I, pp. 492–93.

19. Ha-Levi (1981), pp. 304–5; emphasis added.

20. Ha-Levi does not explicitly mention the three-days yard-stick, but his discussion is based on identifying the patient as "*gosses*"—otherwise the "grain of salt" precedent would not apply.

21. The author explicitly states this in n. 3, p. 303.

22. A powerful critique of attempts to apply the *gosses* category to contemporary medicine is advanced by Sinclair (1989), pp. 9–18. Sinclair proposes instead a novel application of the alternative category of "*terefa*," which denotes terminal organic pathology. He shows some traditional support for killing a person who is *terefa* in order to rescue another person (ibid, ch. 3, "Sacrificing the Life of a '*Terefah*' for the Sake of Preserving Viable Life," pp. 47–69); on this, cf. ch. 4 below.

Sinclair seems to suggest further that it might in general be substantively less grievous to take the life of a *terefa*, and that this is prohibited mainly because of its "side-effects." This suggestion [cited with apparent sympathy by E. Dorff (1991a), at 23 (and n. 52)] depends, however, on a truly bold interpretation of the law. The exemption, in Jewish Law, of a *terefa*'s killer from capital punishment does not indicate an exclusion of such killing from the category of severely forbidden bloodshed. Moved by a basic opposition to capital punishment, the Rabbis introduced numerous exemptions without denying the horror of the deeds or the need for some other punishment; for an extensive discussion, see Pool (1916).

23. See note 10 above. The entire tractate "*Ramat Rachel*" is organized in the form of extended commentaries on clauses from "'*Arukh ha-Shulhan*" by R. Y.M. Epstein. Section 29 is entitled "The Prohibition of Hastening the Death of a *Gosses*, and the Gravity of the Prohibition Against Euthanasia"; its first passage (reproduced here within quotation marks) is from the same source.

24. For an argument against such a sweeping assertion, admitting, however, that in certain cases it may be true, see Brandt (1980). Cf. also Jacobs (1982).

25. For the charges of inconsistency and incoherence which might be leveled at those who oppose suicide on similar theological grounds, see David Hume's essay "Of Suicide." Admittedly, not all of Hume's arguments are fool-proof; see, e.g., the critique by Beauchamp (1976).

26. It is interesting to note that in his letter condemning astrology, Maimonides attributes the disastrous fate of the Jewish polity in the face of Rome to a lack of due military training and preparations. See *Letters of Maimonides*, translated & edited by L.D. Stitskin, New York: Yeshiva University Press, 1977, pp. 119–20.

27. An alternative reading might emphasize instead the metaphor of a gift; see Holly (1989).

28. Within Halakhic discourse, it is sometimes asserted that *Aggadic* sources, that is, non-legal sections of the Talmud or Midrash, can have no authority in determining valid rulings. That this commonly cited formal rule is also frequently disregarded should not come as a great surprise; after all, the values and attitudes expressed in *Aggada* have much to contribute to normative discourse. Still—and quite apart from the issue of authority, which is not our concern here—there is a qualitative difference between a story, which can properly maintain an unresolved tension, and legal writing.

29. A significantly different translation would be: "was extremely afraid of the archers" (but not yet hit).

30. For a rather comprehensive, though not unbiased, survey, see Go'elman (1984).

31. Excluding what might be called a fourth approach which describes Saul's situation as so unique that it can have no relevance to any subsequent predicament. This approach is, I believe, incompatible with the basic *Genesis Rabbah* text, which clearly intends to establish a general permission for cases "like Saul."

32. Other variants of this approach emphasize Saul's role as king; his being captured alive would dishonor Israel and its God or drive the Israelites to desperate suicide missions to liberate their king, costing many more lives. What is common to all these approaches is that what legitimates Saul's taking of his life is not his personal interest in avoiding a protracted and painful death, but (as in martyrdom) some "higher" external interest.

33. See generally Goldstein (1989), pp. 27 ff.

34. See Nahmanides's "*Torat ha-Adam: Sha'ar ha-Hessped*," (Heb., ed. Chavel, 1964, p. 84); cited also in R. Asher ben Yehiel's rulings on tractate *mo'ed qatan*, ch. 3, section 94. The same

position is recorded by R. Joseph Caro in his "Bet Yoseph" annotations to Y.D. 345, s.v. "*ve-khen gadol.*"

The crucial word 'permitted' appears in all these sources; still there are some interesting textual variations. The Midrashic text, as quoted by both Nahmanides and R. Asher, contains an additional descriptive word, *nirdaf* (=pursued), a description of Saul's situation, which is missing from the received text of Gen. Rab. (from the printed editions and manuscripts as well). In addition, R. Asher describes the justifying apprehension as that of being "ravaged" (*mafkirin oto*, lit., "they will do as they wish with him"). Nahmanides, at the same point in his sentence (which R. Asher is citing, or perhaps paraphrasing) characterizes the condition as one of "menace" (*oness*, a term which sometimes, admittedly, signifies compulsion; here the point is, however, not that Saul lacked free will, but rather that he was forced into rationally choosing death).

35. Rabbi Zvi Hirsh's commentary on *shulhan 'arukh* is entitled Bet Lehem Yuhuda. It was first published in 1804 and later incorporated into the standard (Vilna) editions of the code.

36. The author mentions here the proof, cited by *Bet Lehem Yehuda* from Tossafot *gittin* 57b, commenting on a story which commends captured youths for killing themselves [see Goldstein (1989) pp. 42–43]. In a footnote, ben-Shim'on proceeds to wonder why this proof was preferred over Caro's explicit statement exonerating Saul. He answers that whereas Saul was certain of his impending death, the case from *gittin* implies permission for killing oneself without imminent expectation of (otherwise) dying, in order to avoid torture per se. This point has great relevance for the actual case under discussion, as well as for many medical situations.

37. Ben-Shim'on adds, as an auxiliary argument, that "Moreover, there are ample grounds for assuming that she has lost her soundness of mind through the effect of her pains and her lack of any hope of being cured."

38. For an extensive discussion characterizing the debate along similar lines, see Cohn (1984).

39. Member of a contemporary rabbinic court in London.

40. BT *'eruvin* 13b. An alternative translation might be "These and those are the living words of God."

41. Unlike the Christian tradition, which subsumes suicide under "You shall not kill."

42. It would be very helpful eventually to get data from the Netherlands, where euthanasia has been lately legalized; previously, euthanasia in that country was not strictly legal, but was tolerated. There has been some controversy regarding what that experience shows with respect to "slippery slope" concerns. See the various papers addressing this question in the *Hastings Center Report* of March–April 1992, pp. 23–43. For recent observations, see Ciesielski-Carlucci & Kimsma (1994). For an illuminating discussion of the legitimacy versus the potential for fallacy in arguments of this type, see Walton (1992).

3

Parenthood:
Natural Fact and Human Society

I. Is Parenthood Natural?

Our discussion of naturalism thus far has focused on explicitly normative questions. The naturalistic arguments we examined sought to justify a norm by reference to some set of facts. The standard critique of such arguments accepts the posited facts while contesting the proposed inference. For example, suppose the facts are that we can predict the natural pace of death for a suffering patient. From this factual projection, it does not follow, the critique asserts, that the right thing to do is to stand by and let death transpire at some "natural" pace.

The critique of naturalism ought to extend, however, to a more pervasive and subtle naturalistic fallacy, one that involves the facts themselves. For the natural seduces not only through the outright derivation of norms from facts, but also through supposedly "given facts" which set the stage for normative judgments. Many basic values—and markedly those with religious sanction—are enshrined in the social constructs of reality, inducing us to think of some things as "natural" and of their ethical implications as self-evident. Nowhere perhaps is this clearer than in discussions of parenthood, the classical instance of a natural fact with weighty normative significance. Yet the very naturalness of parenthood, along with the self-evidentiary character of its normative implications, is called into question by modern techniques of reproduction. It is to these that we turn in this chapter.

The problems are best introduced by considering discussions about so-called "surrogate motherhood," that is, arrangements by which one woman (the "surrogate mother") undertakes to bear a child for another (the "sponsoring mother") and possibly for the other woman's spouse as well. Sometimes the sponsoring mother supplies the ovum, and after in-vitro fertilization the tiny embryo is implanted in the surrogate for gestation. More commonly, the surrogate mother supplies the ovum as well.

Many discussions of such cases all too quickly adopt the postulate that the woman who biologically produces the child is "*the* mother," or even just take this for granted. The issue is thus decided at the outset, simply by definition: the concept of 'mother', with its host of normative implications, seems inevitably linked to ovulation, fertilization, gestation, and birthing. Its meaning appears to be natural, that is, determined by the (biological) facts, preconstraining normative judgments.

Not surprisingly, some hesitation arises when the possibility of gamete transfer is introduced. Where the surrogate provides only "womb service," two natural elements of motherhood are pitted against each other. Some discussions then tend to take on the character of a factual investigation, aiming to 'discover' which element is the more weighty. In any case, the potential for naturalistic fallacies lies here not so much in any particular deduction or argument, but in the very perception of the task as one of establishing the true *facts* of motherhood (as if we were tissue-testing for paternity).

This description is generally characteristic also of Halakhic essays on surrogate motherhood. Contemporary Halakhic authors tend to perceive their task here as that of determining, on the basis of traditional teachings, how to classify unprecedented realities. A common motif in these discussions therefore is the search for analogies (some from laws pertaining to the animal or vegetable kingdoms) by which, it is expected, the "fact" of true motherhood will be revealed.[1]

The background for this approach lies, in part, in the fact that adoption, the classical model of "parenthood by choice," is not Halakhically recognized as constituting full parenthood.[2] The traditional Halakhic stance conceives of parenthood as a purely natural given. Upon critical consideration, however, this stance is seen as no more value free than other instances of citing the natural as normative. According normative authority to biological facts constitutes a value-laden commitment. This is most plainly revealed in limiting cases, where Halakhic rulings on parenthood deviate from the biological line. The clearest example of this is found in the debate over a practice which is roughly the male counterpart of surrogate motherhood, namely, artificial donor insemination.

II. Artificial Insemination:
Confronting Genetic Paternity

Among modern techniques for enhancing fertility, the oldest and simplest is that of artificial insemination. At times it is employed, utilizing a husband's sperm, to overcome physiological problems in a couple's ability to conceive. Its more common uses, however, have been to circumvent problems of male infertility and, more recently, to facilitate procreation without the involvement of a father.

Artificial Insemination by Donor (initially known as AID and subsequently as simply DI, or Donor Insemination) has been practiced in various countries for more than half a century. Its administration can take one of two basic forms. In one, the sperm of an individual donor is used to fertilize a particular woman, in which case the donor's identity is known, at least to the agent providing the insemination. The alternative is supply from a "sperm bank" where donations are not initially designated for a specific recipient and donor anonymity is preserved.

Donor anonymity is one way of partially coping with the issue of paternity in DI. The donor is basically protected from a paternity suit, while the woman's husband can be registered as father, for the recourse to artificial insemination might be kept secret, known only (say) to the woman, her husband, and to staff at a fertility clinic. Thus the authorities, the child itself, and everyone else will simply assume that the husband is the father even in the biological sense.

Such coping through subterfuge is not, of course, free of problems. The alternative is to openly acknowledge the biological link to the donor, while adopting a non-biological notion of parenthood and recognizing the husband as sole father. This solution was advocated by the Warnock commission[3] and has been enacted in many states.

The prevalent Halakhic position, however, holds to the notion of parenthood as a natural given. Paternity is defined biologically; the father is he whose sperm was employed for fertilization. This position is by no means confined to rulings about artificial insemination; rather, it is reflected in the broad traditional emphasis on lineage (*yihus*). A man's inherited status as *kohen* (=priest), for example,[4] is passed down from father to genetic son, and is not conferred on a boy adopted by a *kohen*. Moreover, the Jewish identity of individuals is itself generally transmitted from parents to children.[5] The prospect of blurred biological paternity in DI thus gives rise to much concern. Waldenberg writes:

> . . . Our Sages forbid bringing about the birth of children whose father is unknown, both because of the requirement that the seed of Israel know their lineage—for otherwise the *Shekhinah* [=Divine Presence] does not dwell upon them—and because of the grievous possibility that this might lead to a situation where a brother marries his paternal [half-]sister...

> . . . It is estimated that one fertile man alone can under certain circumstances sire four hundred children a week, or twenty thousand children over the course of a year! In this shocking situation, ought we not fear that one might very likely come to marry his

paternal sister? Then the earth would be filled, Heaven forbid, with depravity. (*Tsits Eliezer*, IX. 51. iv. ii. 1: pp. 246–47)

Indeed, such wide dissemination of the sperm cells of a single man, with the concomitant risk of unwitting procreation by close relatives, might arouse concern from a genetic-medical viewpoint as well. Accepted practice is, accordingly, to limit the number of inseminations performed from the sperm of any one donor.[6] Waldenberg rightly emphasizes, however, the great stringency of the incest taboo, which may well call for precautions even against low-probability contingencies. This in itself is not implausible; a high degree of caution regarding matters of marriage and "lineage" is an accepted Halakhic norm.[7]

Now this particular problem might be solved by further limitation on the number of women fertilized from any one donor.[8] But the issue of unwitting incest is not, alas, the only problem with DI. For the commitment to genetic paternity entails, for many Halakhists, a different and even more severe pair of problems. With regard to a married woman, DI might be considered adultery and the issuing child illegitimate.

According to one traditional understanding, the prohibition of adultery is expressly meant to prevent X's wife from bearing Y's child. Nahmanides, commenting on one of the biblical verses prohibiting adultery (Lev. 18:20), writes: "Perhaps the Torah says 'for seed'[9] to indicate the reason for the prohibition, for [otherwise] it would not be known of whom the seed is." This leads to a double concern regarding DI. The practice itself might constitute a kind of adultery, and consequently the child might be stigmatized as illegitimate (*mamzer*= one born of adultery or incest).[10]

Waldenberg's response to this concern can, I think, be fairly paraphrased as follows: DI is essentially adulterous, although legally it falls short of being adultery proper. This somewhat complex position is reflected in the dialectical course of his analysis. At the outset, he cites certain earlier rabbis, who considered a married woman receiving

DI an adulteress, and suggested that her child's status thereby also comes under a cloud. Against these extreme rulings, Waldenberg asserts that the formal categories of adultery and illegitimacy, along with the severe sanctions they entail, do not apply to DI. There can be no adultery without illicit sexual relations.

Nevertheless, Waldenberg's ensuing discussion reveals that beyond the letter of the law, he actually endorses the value-judgment behind this same extreme position. Formally, it is true, there is no adultery and therefore no illegitimacy; but in terms of underlying values and principles, DI clearly involves iniquitous sin, which is vigorously denounced:

> The very essence of this matter—namely, placing into the womb of a married woman the seed of another man—is a great abomination in the tents of Jacob, and there is no greater desecration of the family in the dwelling places of Israel. This destroys all the sublime concepts of purity and holiness of Jewish family life, for which our people has been so noted since it became a nation . . . (ibid., Ch. 5, sec. 1, p. 251)

Any effort to furnish a more lenient ruling, motivated by compassion for a childless couple, he goes on to argue, would be utterly misplaced. A child born from DI will not bring true happiness to the home. On the contrary, as the child develops, it will be a growing source of estrangement and anguish. Waldenberg tersely warns, in this context, of the resultant "destruction of the family" (ibid); this warning should be read as an allusion to a fuller exposition in an essay by another rabbinic author, sympathetically quoted by Waldenberg:

> Let us portray their catastrophe: thus far they did not have a child, while now they have found relief and produced a child. But let us see who will rejoice in this child: she has prevailed against her husband, who agreed to her receiving into her body the seed of a

non-Jew.[11] But immediately when her pregnancy shows, there will be a great crisis in their family life. The husband knows and is aware that within her a fetus is being formed, in which he has no part or share . . .[12]

It is instructive to note how the biological conception of parenthood, with a peculiarly patriarchal twist, is given normative force. The wife seems willing to endorse a non-naturalistic norm of parenthood. The child will be biologically related to her but not to her husband; yet she is inviting him to jointly raise the child. The husband will, however, naturally (and, these rabbis imply, rightly) find it hard to experience love toward the stranger's child developing within his own wife's body.[13] DI is described here as the wife's unilateral initiative. The husband's 'consent' is therefore perceived as reluctant capitulation, which will surely be insufficient to overcome the alienation he must feel toward the child from the very beginning.[14]

III. An Alternate View: Beyond Biology

M. Feinstein, the major spokesman for the position permitting DI, also starts from a conception of biological paternity. Although he shares the Halakhic postulate that the father is the donor, he sees nothing fundamentally wrong with X's wife bearing Y's child. A woman's marital commitment involves sexual fidelity only, not restriction of her reproductive capacity. While for Waldenberg DI constitutes reproductive infidelity and therefore amounts to quasi-adultery, Feinstein considers it to be wholly within the wife's rights. He cites[15] with strong disagreement a position akin to Waldenberg's:

The statement . . . that "Heaven forbid that a daughter of Israel should abandon herself to the artificial adultery invented by the physicians" is mere rhetoric, for this has no connection to adultery whatever. (*Iggerot Moshe, Even ha-'Ezer* 71)

The term 'artificial adultery' reflects the view that DI for a married woman constitutes substantive infidelity to her husband. The artificial mode of this 'adultery', that is, lack of sexual intercourse, may mitigate against applying the severest sanctions, but it cannot obscure the abhorrent character of the deed: "Heaven forbid that she should abandon herself . . ."

Against this, Feinstein asserts that DI "has no connection to adultery whatever."[16] Even when stipulating a requirement for the husband's consent, he is careful to ground it exclusively in the indirect effects upon what he takes to be a spouse's legitimate interests:

> But without the husband's consent it is not permitted, because she is bound to her husband. For when she is pregnant it is often impossible for the husband to have intercourse with her when he wishes. He also may not wish to take care during intercourse as is required with a pregnant woman. Besides, this will cause him great expenses: she has no right to cause him the excessive expenses of pregnancy and delivery and the expenses connected with a child . . . (ibid., p. 170)

For Feinstein too, a married woman is not entirely autonomous. But there is no restriction upon her reproductive freedom *per se*; rather, her use of that freedom is limited by its impingement on her obligations in other realms.[17] The harm to the husband in her pregnancy is indirect, somewhat like the monetary cost he incurs, assuming him to be the main property owner and breadwinner. The clear implication is that, had the couple agreed upon separation for a period of a year—for example, in order to earn a living—the husband could have no valid objection to his wife's pregnancy by artificial insemination during the course of that year.

Feinstein's approach is expressed even more clearly in his attitude toward DI with the husband's consent. Such consent is not viewed as given grudgingly, a surrender to the wife's obstinance, but as true participation. For crucial to Feinstein's lenient ruling is the consideration for the infertile couple's plight, "in a situation of great distress, when *they* are very much pained in *their* desire for a child" (ibid, emphases added). Indeed, the plural pronoun reflects a perception of the husband's relation to the prospective child quite distinct from that warranted by the purely biological definition of paternity. Legally it is the donor who is the child's father, and yet the husband significantly regards it as his own, as fulfilling the desire for a child shared with his wife.

Still, the legal affirmation of biological paternity combined with donor anonymity continues to raise the specter of marriage between unsuspecting half-siblings. Here Feinstein takes a further step away from strict biological parenthood. Presuming the donor to be non-Jewish, his solution utilizes the general Halakhic ruling which refuses to recognize paternity in mixed procreation; where only one of the parents is Jewish, traditional Halakha regards the child as having only a mother.[18] Thus the children of two Jewish women inseminated by sperm from the same non-Jewish donor are not legally siblings.

Obviously the legal denial of paternity is frequently at odds with emotional and social reality. This gap between legal pronouncements and human reality is aptly expressed by B.H. 'Uziel (Chief Rabbi of Israel, mid-twentieth century). 'Uziel ruled that a Jewish man must support children which he has by a non-Jewish mother, even though he is not Halakhically their father, for "though they are not his sons, still they are his children!"[19]

In the case of DI, however, the denial of paternity on technical grounds is complemented by the donor's intentional severance of any link to the child. On the emotional-social plane, the fathering is already discharged by the woman's spouse. The remaining link to the donor is, on this view, merely a legal hurdle, properly surmounted by a legal ruse. This leaves the way clear for Feinstein's recognition of the emotional reality of paternity by consent.

An additional step away from a strictly genetic definition of parenthood is represented in 'Uziel's own discussion of artificial insemination (*Mishpetei 'Uziel, Even ha-'Ezer* 19). This author's unique approach is reflected in the title he gives to that discussion, "Artificial Pregnancy." A pregnancy induced by artificial insemination, although it progresses normally and produces a child, lacks the natural basis for paternity—sexual intercourse—and is therefore itself "artificial." By thus diminishing the significance of (male) genetic contribution, 'Uziel reaches a remarkable conclusion: that a child born of DI[20] is like one born through parthenogenesis, having no father at all.

Formally, this approach is an instance of naturalism, since the pregnancy's origin is denied moral significance by virtue of being artificial. It is, however, not the *biological fact* of fertilization, but the *human act* of intercourse, which is identified as natural. The impersonal character of artificial insemination directly excludes imputations of donor paternity, so that there is no need to resort to the device of employing a non-Jewish donor. The mere contribution of genetic material has no normative significance outside the framework of human action.

This ruling, which emphasizes action above genetics, might contain the kernel of a more radical proposal. If 'Uziel's radical approach to artificial insemination is endorsed, then it is at least arguable that we should recognize additional human acts as establishing parenthood. Specifically, this might apply to the series of human acts of fathering performed by a woman's spouse, and, by the same token, to adoptive parenthood in general. The final section of this chapter discusses options of parenthood based on human initiative: adoption and surrogate motherhood.

IV. Surrogate Motherhood and Adoption:
Transcending Nature

In the context of DI, we addressed the issue of personal autonomy in connection with the wife of an infertile man. What might be the analogous concern in the context of surrogacy arrangements, where the husband of an infertile woman seeks to reproduce through the contribution of another woman? It might be thought that Halakhic concern here would again focus on marital fidelity, castigating extra-marital procreation. The same authors who strictly forbid a married woman to avail herself of DI ought, it seems, to similarly forbid a married man to procreate with any woman other than his wife.

Actually we find nothing of the kind, and for a simple, if disconcerting, reason: namely, because the Halakhic tradition relating to marriage is far from egalitarian. Under biblical and Rabbinic law, a man could have many wives or concubines, and the Hebrew term *ni'uf*, commonly translated as "adultery," in fact refers exclusively to infidelity committed by a married *woman* (and by her lover, regardless of his marital status), never to unfaithfulness by a married man. Even after the tenth-century ban on polygamy, the marital bonds and restrictions in Jewish law are far from reciprocal.[21]

Admittedly, the rabbinic traditions with respect to the status of women are far from uniform; in other aspects of marital law, such as those pertaining to economic relations, they are much more egalitarian.[22] A critique of Halakhic inequalities need not, therefore, be solely external, drawing on a contemporary Western commitment to gender equality; rather, it could find internal grounds as well.[23] Any corrective move might, in theory, at least, take either of two dichotomous forms. On the one hand, wives' freedom could be enhanced to emulate their husbands' relatively free access to other female partners. Or conversely, following in the footsteps of medieval legislation, the standards for male sexual fidelity could be raised to match those traditionally applied to wives.

It should come as no surprise that notions of "open marriage" hold scarce appeal for traditionally-minded Jews; regarding sexual intimacy, only the second of these alternatives will be perceived as acceptable. Regarding procreation, however, the options are open, and the debate on DI ought arguably to extend to surrogacy as well. But this is not the case. As noted above, Halakhic discussions of surrogacy seem to concentrate on "discovering" who the real mother is,[24] expressing little concern over the husband's "procreational infidelity." Here there appears to be wide acceptance of a view analogous to Feinstein's, endorsing (male) reproductive freedom.

A husband's freedom to reproduce with a woman other than his wife is not, however, sufficient to yield what is the commonly desired result, namely, granting maternal status to the wife. It might be suggested that this need not be granted through outright denial of the surrogate's maternity. Instead, a more conventional solution seems to suffice; the baby, once born, can be simply handed over in adoption. This, however, would seem to completely rule out commercial surrogacy, for if a woman is paid in exchange for giving over her baby for adoption, does this not constitute illicit baby-selling?

As argued cogently by Shalev (1989), commercial surrogacy contracts can only escape the charge of "baby selling" by virtue of redefining motherhood on the basis of personal autonomy. Any payment received is strictly for the service of gestation, not for the transfer of parental rights, for these are here, from the very beginning, not determined by the biological connection. The "true" mother is, on this view, the woman who initiated the generation of this baby. It is she who has undertaken to be this child's mother, not the surrogate mother who, by her own self-determination, has contracted to deliver it for her.

The notion of motherhood as an undertaking, determined by choice rather than by biological facts, is analogous to the notion we approached at the end of our discussion with regard to fatherhood in the previous section. Ultimately, such a notion of parenthood must draw on the model of adoption.

The Halakhic tradition, however, like several other legal systems and traditions, holds parenthood to be nontransferable.[25] The parental relation is perceived as a natural link determined by the genetic facts of procreation. Although it is sometimes possible, as we saw, for that link to be severed by the force of normative considerations,

Halakha has not granted legal validity to the converse possibility, namely, that of parental relations constituted by
human commitment.

Notwithstanding this legal position, the rabbis were
familiar with the social and emotional realities of children
being raised by persons—designated "guardians"—other
than their genetic parents. The sources on this issue are
cited and discussed extensively by Gold (1988, pp. 153–61),
and there is no need to canvas them here. In one text, a
guardian leads the orphan he has raised to her wedding
canopy, and she asks that his name be recorded as her
father in the marriage documents, "Because I know of no
other father save you." The rabbinic source, which tells
this story as a parable, concludes: ". . . he that brings up a
child is called a father, not he that begets." (Ex. Rab. 46:5).

Gold goes on to say that "Judaism has a long history
of adoption de facto," and mentions as well some recent
rabbinic efforts to bring the legal situation closer to what
exists in fact. But it is also worth emphasizing the theological point of the parable. Israel's relationship to God,
as their adoptive father, supersedes their relationship to
the natural ancestor Abraham.[26] God Himself is father not
genetically, of course, but only through adoption. Here,
the relationship to the divine is founded on a model of
transcending the natural.

This theological perspective matches the Maimonidean
approach depicted above (in Chapter 1). The naturally
given is not definitive of the way God wills things to be.
Where the given reality is unsatisfactory, it is appropriate
for human beings to intervene in order to try and make
things better.

Whether assisted reproduction actually makes things
better is not, of course, a simple question. Each form of
such reproduction (donor insemination, surrogacy, ovum
donation, etc.) involves various social and moral issues.
These issues would have to be addressed for each method
to determine whether it is worthy or even acceptable. All I
can do here is to examine those considerations connected to
naturalism. What, then, does the legitimacy of transcending

the natural imply regarding assisted reproduction?

Minimally, it implies that assisted reproduction should not be condemned merely for being "unnatural." As suggested by the parable of divine adoption, it sometimes can be proper and valuable to transcend natural relationships. But is there room, in the Halakhic tradition, for full validation of parenthood by consent?

As we have seen, the main tendency among Halakhic authors has been toward re-emphasizing parenthood as a naturally given link. But with regard to the male genetic link, we have also noted significant exceptions. This suggests that the affirmation of biological parenthood and the concomitant invalidation of parenthood by consent reflect a value-commitment rather than an inevitable necessity.

Notes

1. See, e.g., Broyde (1988).

2. See section IV below.

3. Warnock (1985), p. 85 ("Recommendations," section E: Legal Changes, #51–52 =Paragraphs 4.17 and 4.22).

4. The status of *kohen* has ramifications in some details of synagogue ritual, as well as in certain restrictions in marital options.

5. Traditional Halakha defines matrilineal descent, while contemporary Reform policy extends Jewish lineage to patrilineal descent as well. In addition, of course, persons without any Jewish lineage can convert to Judaism; arguably, this possibility might suggest an analogous notion of parenthood based on choice.

6. The Warnock commission recommended a limit of ten; see Warnock (1985), p. 82 ("Recommendations," section B: Principles of Provision, #23 =Paragraph 4.26).

7. Expressed in the dictum "a higher standard was established in matters of lineage" (e.g., BT *qiddushin* 73a, MT Laws of Forbidden Intercourse 15:21).

8. The non-genetic redefinition of paternity in DI may facilitate an alternative solution. Insofar as it renders donor anonymity superfluous, marriage of unsuspecting close relatives should be effectively prevented.

9. The text reads: "Do not have carnal relations with (*titen shekhovtekha le-zara'*, lit., 'lie with . . . for seed') your neighbor's wife and defile yourself with her."

10. A *mamzer* is barred, under Halakha, from marriage to most persons. The inherent injustice of the *mamzer* law, which penalizes the offspring for the sins of their parents, has long been recognized in Halakhic literature. Analysis of the various traditional responses to this must remain, however, outside the scope of the present work.

11. The reason for referring to the sperm donor as a "non-Jew" will become apparent in the following section. In any case, it seems that the author would expect the husband to have much the same feelings toward "alien seed" of another Jew.

12. R. Sh. Halberstam, "*Ma'amar le- hatsalat yihus u-kedushat yisrael*" (="An essay for Saving the Holiness and Lineage of Israel"), *ha-Ma'or*, 1964/65; emphasis added.

13. For a similar argument attacking AID as "self-contradictory" see R. Chadwick's introduction, "Having Children," in R. Chadwick (ed., 1987), pp. 3–43. The psychological assessment expressed here turns out, however, to be empirically quite dubious; see Snowden et al (1983) for an illuminating study.

14. Rabbi Waldenberg summarizes his position thus: "It is forbidden to fertilize a married woman with the seed of another man by means of artificial insemination; such a deed is a great abomination and very evil. Indeed some [rabbis] tend towards the view that a married woman who does so is even forbidden to her husband." (Ibid., Summary, p. 258)

15. Giving the reference: the argument is "cited in *Otzar ha-Poskim* from the book *Menahem Meshiv*."

16. The expression "mere rhetoric" (*devarim be-'alma*) is a polite form of dismissal. At face value, the statement is plain wrong; in order to avoid attributing a bold error to his distinguished disputant, Feinstein suggests a forced interpretation of the term *zenut* as a term of contempt.

17. The term 'being bound' (Hebrew, *shi'abud*) is taken from the realm of civil law, where it implies something approximating 'lien'.

18. According to one rabbinic commentator, the child's identity is determined by its primary bond to the mother, with the link to the father, whether Jewish or non-Jewish, curtailed in the name of cultural consistency. See Rabbi B.H. 'Uziel, *Mishpetei 'Uziel*, YD 60, pp. 205–6.

19. Ibid, p. 210.

20. Apparently, this applies even to a child produced by artificial insemination from semen of the woman's own spouse!

21. See generally Falk (1962).

22. For an illuminating analysis, see Morrell (1982).

23. I attempted something along such lines in Zohar (1993a).

24. Especially when there are two candidates for motherhood on biological grounds, a "gestational mother" vs. a "genetic mother."

25. Muslim law, e.g., equally denies that adoption can effect a transfer of parenthood; the same was true of English law prior to 1926.

26. Hermeneutically the point is to provide an explanation for two verses quoted from Isaiah (64:7 as well as 63:16).

God and Nature: A Summary

The relationship to God is unquestionably central to the Halakhic normative system. But, as shown by the foregoing discussions, the specific impact of the divine on human affairs is far from unequivocal.

The Nahmanidean view emphasizes utter trust and reliance; its ideal is human dependence upon God, whose main influence in the ethical sphere tends, on this view, to be one of restraint. The focal issue of religious ethics becomes, in consequence, the setting of boundaries to human endeavor. Human efforts are to be limited by the Creator's will, and this will is revealed not only in normative discourse, but also in facts of nature.

In the Halakhic tradition, however, this credo of religious naturalism is countered by a perception of human intervention as itself divinely mandated. With respect to the practice of medicine in general, the contemporary Halakhic trend is indeed pro-intervention, despite medieval reservations (voiced by several eminent commentators) against fully embracing medicine. Still, in specific medical contexts, the force of religious naturalism continues to be felt.

In the discussion of euthanasia, we witnessed the rabbinic condemnation of suicide and the deontological reverence at the death-bed reflected in medieval sources. Rabbi Waldenberg, drawing on these traditions, insists that determining the time for a person's death is in God's exclusive domain. This insistence is shared by quite a few writers in recent years.[1] But in the Halakhically endorsed setting of contemporary interventionist medicine, it hardly seems possible to sincerely and consistently exclude human control at the end of life. Normative judgments about continuation or shortening of suffering are unavoidable and are clearly in keeping with important strands in the tradition. Once the need for normative choice is recognized, it becomes virtually untenable to fall back on natural processes as clear indications of God's will.

A much broader scope of religious naturalism can be discerned in judgments which appear, at first glance, to involve no normative aspects but merely facts. Traditional views of parenthood seem to perceive its biological base as self-evident and immutable. Yet the character of parenthood as a social institution, subject to cultural determination, is seen in the traditional rule about interfaith procreation. Rabbinic literature also sometimes expresses recognition of the real parental bonds formed in adoptive relationships.

These two departures from the biological conception of parenthood complement each other, together suggesting that the extent of naturalistic determination can be subject to normative appraisal and possible adjustment. Hence, insofar as "natural" parenthood is retained as a guiding principle in decisions about new reproductive technologies, this should be recognized as itself the product of human resolution. Just as at the end of life, so too at its conception, natural processes can describe divine limits only through human designation.

The examples of euthanasia and of parenthood do not, of course, exhaust the practical expressions of religious naturalism. Still they are sufficient to illustrate the effects, in the context of bioethics, of focusing on God as the One who establishes the boundaries of human initiative. They present the continued force of religious naturalism as well as the problems it necessarily faces within a tradition that has, overall, embraced human responsibility.

Relating to God as author of limitations is not, however, the only—nor even the most important—religious aspect of Halakhic ethics. At least as important, and, it seems, less prone to inherent contradictions, is the fundamental belief that every human being is created in God's image. This symbolic faith is the kernel of Halakhic religious humanism, which is the theme of Part II. After exploring the significance of "in God's image" in basic Rabbinic sources, we shall go on to examine three bioethical issues pertaining to Jewish religious humanism.

Note

1. I discussed this trend in some detail in Zohar (1993c).

PART II

Religious Humanism

Elements of Religious Humanism

This section is intended as a brief exposition of the Rabbinic belief that human beings are created in God's image. This core idea of Rabbinic religious humanism is then related to the bioethical discussions that constitute Part II of the book.

As a point of departure, let us look at a traditional distinction between two normative realms. The distinction appears in a statement about atonement which contrasts two types of transgressions:

> The Day of Atonement effects atonement for transgressions between a person and God. As for transgressions between one person and another—The Day of Atonement does not effect atonement, unless [the transgressor] first appeases the other. (Mishna *yoma* 8:9)

Clearly, both types of transgressions are perceived as sins for which the transgressor seeks atonement from God. This is straightforward enough in the first type, where the aggrieved party and the author of atonement are one and the same. With regard to the second type, however, the picture is a bit more complex. The aggrieved party is another person, whose forgiveness must be sought, but once that is attained, what further need is there for atonement?

One simple answer is that God underwrites the requirements of interpersonal morality, so that in hurting another person one also sins before God. Such divine back-

ing does not affect the character of these moral requirements; it only invests them with additional authority.
Therefore, even if their spirit is humanistic, they do not
constitute a distinctly religious humanism but simply a
humanistic ethic religiously endorsed.

Comparison with other Rabbinic sources, however,
suggests another reading of the relation between the two
normative realms, that "between a person and God" and
that "between one person and another." The following text
is a commentary on the concrete form of the Ten Commandments, which were inscribed on two tablets constituting, our text presumes, two columns of five. Employing the classification we encountered above, it may roughly
be said that the second tablet is devoted to commandments "between one person and another," while the first
contains those "between a person and God."

> How were the Ten Commandments presented? Five
> on one tablet and five on the other. Scripture pro-
> nounces "You shall have no other God"—and facing
> that, "You shall not kill." Scripture thus pronounces
> that anyone who sheds blood is considered as though
> he had diminished the [divine] Image.
>
> A parable: [This is] like a king who entered a state,
> set up icons, produced statues, and minted coins [all
> with his likeness]. After some time, the [people] over-
> turned the icons, broke the statues and defaced the
> coins—[thereby] diminishing the king's image.
> Similarly, anyone who sheds blood is considered as
> though he had diminished the [divine] image, as writ-
> ten, "Whoever sheds the blood of a human, by human
> [hands] shall his blood be shed, for in God's image
> was the human made." (Gen. 9:6). (Mekhilta *ba-
> hodesh* 8)

The text goes on down the twin columns, expounding the
substantive connections between the pairs of commandments. Here the relation between religious commitment

and interpersonal morality goes clearly beyond plain endorsement, taking the form of a complex, interwoven fabric. Does this amount to religious humanism? To answer that question, let us dwell on how the parable illuminates the notion of "diminishing the image."

When a human being is attacked, says our text, this constitutes an assault on God's image. Yet, on one reading, the parable's message is rather *anti*-humanistic, for icons and statues have little value in themselves; their true value derives from what they represent, being symbols of the king's realm. Human beings are thus valued—to draw the parallel—merely as emblems of God; the severity of killing a person lies in the damage inflicted on God's domain. In Kantian terms it might be said that human beings are valued here not as ends in themselves, but as means for promoting God's image.

This understanding of the Rabbinic commentary on the Ten Commandments is in turn at variance with the statement regarding atonement. For if the evil in harming a person is only the offense it offers to God, then all Halakhic norms dissolve into the category of "transgressions between a person and God," and seeking atonement before God ought to be a fully sufficient remedy. Surely it would be quite odd if the people in the parable, repenting, let us suppose, and seeking to attain forgiveness, should proceed to mollify the fallen icons.[1]

An alternative understanding of the parable that is more in harmony with the doctrine on atonement is suggested by a striking embellishment of the coin metaphor, found in a third Rabbinic text. This text is part of a homily on the value of human life included in the Mishna's record of the "warning" addressed to prospective witnesses in capital cases. The homily is arranged as a string of explanations for the fact that God chose to create, as the beginning of the human race, a single person. And one answer is that this comes

to show the greatness of the Holy One. For a person mints many coins with one stamp, and they are all the same. But the King of Kings, the Holy One, mints every person in the mint of the first Adam, and not one of them is the same as another. Therefore, every person ought to say: The world was created for me. (Mishna *sanhedrin* 4:5).

The metaphor has been given a paradoxical twist implying a crucial shift in the locus of value. The value of actual coins depends on their being "all the same," whereby they reflect that which is external to them as mere objects. In a monarchy they carry the king's image, reflecting the power of the sovereign. The divine "coins," by contrast, derive their value, like collector's items, each from its uniqueness. Yes, each person is valued as an image of God, but, as with a work of art, the form cannot be subtracted from the content: each image is unique in him or her self. Unlike ordinary coins or icons, people are not mere symbols of a transcendent divine entity; rather, the human mosaic *constitutes* the divine image.[2]

This is indeed a version of humanism: inherent value is ascribed to every human being. But it is a religious humanism whose valuations are at least partly conceived in terms of theistic symbolism. As we noted above in the discussion of euthanasia, such valuations may inform deontological prohibitions which will not necessarily coincide with the interests of the persons involved. For some rabbis, as a matter of fact, this religious humanism even generates obligations where no human interest is at stake:

R. El'azar b. 'Azaria says: Anyone who does not engage in procreation, is considered as though he had diminished the [divine] image. (Tosefta *yevamot* 8:7)

Surely, failing to procreate cannot constitute harm to the interests of those people not created. This is not only because it is debatable whether living in this world should be thought a benefit,[3] but also more importantly because as long as a person is not created there is no one to have the interest in coming to exist.[4] These nebulous considerations are, however, beside R. El'azar's point: he is speaking of harm not to unborn people but to the divine image. His statement is hyperbolic, for it equates failure to enhance the image with actually diminishing it, but the idea itself is perfectly understandable, given the notion of a humanism that transcends the interests of human beings.

This perspective is extremely helpful for appreciating Halakhic attitudes toward birth control. On the one hand, neither contraception nor even abortion are equated to killing, except in hyperbole;[5] the taboo on taking a human life applies only from the moment of birth onwards.[6] On the other hand, preventing the birth of a human being is conceived as an evil in itself tantamount to "diminishing the divine image." These two premises tend, of course, to carry conflicting implications for practice, and we should not be surprised to find a rather wide range of disparate Halakhic teachings on these matters. There is no need, however, to canvas these teachings here, as this task has already been fulfilled quite adequately by D. Feldman.[7]

In the following chapters, we shall focus instead on two other expressions of the religious humanism of the Jewish tradition. In terms of the ongoing dialogue with Western bioethics, these will lead us in two rather different directions.

First, we shall examine some of the problems involved in choosing between lives, from within a framework which accords nearly absolute value to each and every human life. In Chapter 4, we shall thus discuss the question of numbers and of "life-years," as well as (again) the distinction between killing and not saving. Here I shall endeavor to give a philosophical account of a certain Halakhic conception of concrete, individual duty. In addition, the humanistic doctrine of "divine image" will be invoked in criticizing certain non-egalitarian strands of the Halakhic tradition.

Second, we shall look in Chapter 5 at the special Halakhic regard for the human dead, comparing it to some basic postulates of modern norms pertaining to cadavers and to their use in medical training and research. Philosophical analysis of the Halakhic debate here leads to an examination of the relation between ends and means. An unsettling Halakhic dichotomy may be overcome, I will suggest, through appreciating the philosophical notion of "role morality."

In conjunction, the concerns of these two chapters lay the foundation for our final issue, social allocation of medical resources. In Chapter 6, we will examine a pivotal argument which exemplifies some of the limitations inherent to the individualistic strand of Halakhic ethics. In this argument, we shall again encounter a tendency to curtail human responsibility, explicitly relying on the Nahmanidean tradition of religious naturalism.

Notes

1. It would, however, make perfect sense for them to begin by raising back the icons. Similarly, redressing the harm done to the wronged person would be a plausible precondition for gaining divine forgiveness, even under an entirely theocentric ethic. But a cognate source clearly indicates that the Rabbis' concern went beyond this, that they conceived of interpersonal wrongs as transgressions toward the other person. In the concluding paragraph of the Mishna chapter dealing with assault we read, "Even though he pays him, he [=the culprit] is not forgiven until he petitions him [=the victim]," etc. (Mishna *bava qama* 8:7).

2. Lest we fall afoul of traditional theology, it is worth noting that God's *Image* is by no means identical to God, who is Himself, of course, not "constituted" by His reflections (or by anything else).

3. This was in fact hotly debated amongst the Rabbis, with the final consensus being negative; see BT *'eruvin* 13b.

4. This was argued extensively by David Heyd (1992); see also Zohar (1991).

5. Most notably, in BT *sanhedrin* 57b; a source often cited in contemporary Halakhic writing to support assertions that abortion is "tantamount to bloodshed."

6. Mishna *niddah* 5:3; and cf. also *ohalot* 7:6 and BT *'arakhin* 7a.

7. Feldman (1968, 1974); see also Bleich (1977), vol. I, 325 ff.

4

Human Life, Human Lives:
Assessing the Absolute

I. Equality of Persons: Rava's Basic Ruling

Humanism, as commonly understood, involves valuing each individual *qua* human being, and hence implies a commitment to human equality.[1] Certainly that is the sense of the coin parable cited above. Each individual is a unique reflection of the divine image, and in this is fundamentally equal to every other person.

In the context of medical practice, we find the equality-of-persons ideal most ardently asserted (and yet sometimes contested) when choices must be made between lives. Such choices generally involve a shortage of drugs and equipment, the time and energy of trained personnel, or human-body resources (from organs to reproductive functions). There are, of course, important differences in the mode and context of the competition for these things. But rather than begin by imposing some scheme of distinctions, I propose to work them out in the course of examining the scope of the commitment to equality.

For an initial formulation, let us consider a rhetorical question cited in a classical talmudic discussion. The issue being discussed is not directly medical; the Talmud is seeking to establish why fear of death cannot justify murder.

And how do we know that, concerning bloodshed, one should be killed rather than transgress? It stands to reason, as in [the case] with Rava. For a person came before Rava (a fourth century sage), and said:

> "The master of my town has said to me:
> 'Go kill so-and-so; if you don't, I shall kill you'!"
> He replied: "Let him kill you and do not kill.
> **Who is to say that your blood is redder—
> perhaps his blood is redder?**"[2]

This 'redness of blood' is not meant to denote personal vigor; the figure of speech derives from biblical imagery, which emphasizes the crimson stain of bloodguilt. Rava's question focuses on a comparison of value. Who is to say that the loss of the one life would be a greater disaster than the loss of the other?

In fact, we can imagine various arguments by which the man might have tried to assert that his life was somehow worth more. After all, there is a hierarchical strand in the Jewish tradition; perhaps he could claim superiority of ancestry or of current religious standing.[3] Or, on more familiar grounds, he might have pointed out that he was much younger than the prospective victim, so that his own death would mean a loss of far more "life years." But Rava's pointed retort was designed precisely to forestall such arguments, emphasizing the fundamental equality of persons.

The moral force of Rava's reason seems to have prevented counter-arguments in post-talmudic times as well. After all, in the classical Halakhic mode of commentary to the Talmud, it would have been quite easy, in terms of formal legality, to qualify Rava's ruling, that is, to stipulate that it applied only if the persons involved are indeed equals, but not if they are in some relevant sense non-equals. As we shall see, some medieval commentators argued in just this way regarding cumulative value of human lives, implying that the blood of the many is "redder" than the blood of an individual. Yet I know of no attempt to qualify Rava's ruling in terms of differences between individuals, however valid such differences may be considered in other contexts.

II. Equality: The Case for Random Selection

Applied to questions of allocating scarce resources for saving life, this commitment to the equality of persons seems to imply a refusal to prefer any one potential patient over another. Thus J.F. Childress (1983), among many others, advocates "random selection" as affording "equality of opportunity," with an important addition regarding the form of its implementation:

> My proposal is that we extend this principle (first come, first served) to determine who among the medically acceptable patients shall live or that we utilize artificial chance such as a lottery or randomness. "First come, first served" would be more feasible than a lottery since the applicants make their claims over a period of time rather than as a group at one time.[4]

Admittedly, this Queue Policy (first come, first served) is a less than perfect approximation of an organized lottery or pure random selection. Childress calls the queue "natural chance," but it is only partly natural, inasmuch as the applicants arrive in the order in which they contract the life-threatening disease. In fact, differentials in education, urban geography, and similar factors which are more social than natural—will surely have an effect on the very formation of the queue.

Perhaps, however, a queue's deviation from true randomness is set off by what Childress calls "feasibility," that is, the fact that the queue forms of itself without the need to organize a special agency with its own bureaucracy. Under this assumption, the Queue Policy is an acceptable approximation of random selection, and we shall regard it as such.

Adherents of the equality principle sharply criticize alternative procedures of deliberate selection, which by some "rational measures" endeavor to choose whose life should be preferred. Those who exercise such rational choice are accused of "playing God," and the famous dialysis selection committee in Seattle was even nicknamed the God Committee. The argument, it seems, is not so much that only God ought to have authority to decide matters of life and death—for, after all, some decision must be made by humans—but rather that only God (if anyone)

may judge the relative values of human lives. Human deliberation exceeds its legitimate scope once it departs from
ascribing basic equality.[5]

Not infrequently, this position is supported by comparison to a hypothetical proposal to terminate the treatment of any given patient in order to facilitate treatment of
another, arguably more deserving, person. If criteria for
choosing between persons were allowed, would this not
imply that a physician might be right in walking up to a
patient in a hospital ward and, while disconnecting the
respirator, announcing, "Sorry, this respirator is needed
for another patient"?!

This (supposedly unanswerable) question is invoked in
order to show the inconsistency, and thereby the patent
absurdity, of any principle of rational selection.[6] If we were
to accept criteria for rational choice regarding whom to
save, we would be bound, on this view, to follow the same
criteria in further transferring our limited resources from
those initially selected to yet more appropriate candidates.
Conversely, as long as we share Rava's principle and forbid
terminating[7] one life in order to procure the continuance of
another, we must equally eschew any criteria for initial
selection between prospective patients.

III. Halakhic Approaches:
Against Lottery, Permitting Choice

Given Rava's undisputed principle of equality, we
might expect a similar tendency in the Jewish tradition.
Indeed, F. Rosner (1983a,b) states categorically that "the
(*sic!*) Jewish view" calls for "selection based on chance,
such as a first-come, first-served rule or selection by lot."
This is, at best, true only in part. As we shall see, a strong
case is made in contemporary Halakhic writing for a certain version of a Queue Policy, yet it is emphatically *not*
based on a commitment to chance selection or to strict
equality.

In fact, despite its commitment to Rava's ruling, the
Jewish tradition reflects a contrary tendency toward mak-

ing certain deliberate choices between lives. The apparent paradox in this dual approach can, I shall argue in section V below, be resolved by assuming a particular conception of our duty to save others. But first, let us illustrate the approach which sanctions deliberate choice through another Talmudic paragraph, which relates an ancient disagreement:

> This case has been discussed:
>
> Two people are walking [in a desert], and one has a canteen with water; if they both drink [of it], they will die; if [only] one drinks, he will reach civilization.
>
> Ben-Patura taught: Best that they both drink and die, so none witness the other's death.
>
> Finally Rabbi 'Akiva taught: "that your brother may live with you" (Lev. 25:35)—your life takes precedence over his life. (BT *bava metsi'a* 62a)

In Ben-Patura's view, for one traveler to drink the water alone, thereby ensuring the death of the other, is impermissible. The person in possession of the water may not prefer his own life any more than may the threatened person in Rava's case; who is to say that his blood is redder?

As implied in the language of the talmudic passage ("*Finally* Rabbi 'Akiva taught"), it is Rabbi 'Akiva's view that has become accepted in the Halakhic tradition. Since Rava's ruling, too, has remained undisputed, systematization of Talmudic Law calls for an account of why self-preference is allowed in one situation ("Your life takes precedence") while prohibited in the other ("Who is to say that your blood is redder?").

The straightforward answer seems to be that Rava's ruling prohibits saving oneself by murdering another, while R. 'Akiva relates only to "witnessing the other's death." But is there a convincing moral difference here between killing and letting die? The commission/omission distinction was discussed extensively above in Chapter 2. There, in the context of euthanasia, I expressed persistent doubt regarding its moral significance. Nevertheless, I will propose an account of the difference between killing and letting die in the present context of moral conflict.

Even if the severity of moral, or even legal, liability one incurs by an omission is fully equated to that incurred through a commission, there remains an essential condition which must be met in order for an omission to be defined in the first place. An omission can only be defined against the background of a posited duty. This is a commonplace in legal discussions of omission; it becomes clear once we think, for example, of a parent's liability for letting his or her child die through neglect. The omission does not consist merely in the fact that the parent failed to provide the child with crucial nourishment; after all, many other people equally failed to do so. But the parent, unlike others, had a special duty to provide for this child. It is the breach of this duty which constitutes the culpable omission.

With regard to moral liability, this may seem at first glance to be merely a fine point of sophistry. Granted that letting die can be deemed tantamount to killing only on the basis of a duty to rescue, does not every person have a general duty to save the life of any other? In the case of the two travelers specifically, it would seem that the one with the canteen has a *prima facia* obligation to rescue his fellow. If he fails to do so, claiming the 'necessity' of saving his own life, how is he different from one who would kill in order to save himself?

This can be answered, I believe, in terms of the analytical truth that 'ought' implies 'can', that is, that the scope of our duties is limited by the scope of our capabilities. If I have no water, I have no duty to save your life by giving you water. By the same token, once it is stipulated that the person with the canteen may drink the water himself, there is no more water available, and thus he cannot be said to have a duty to save his fellow's life.

This reasoning may appear to be circular, but the converse approach is no less circular, namely, positing a duty of rescue based on a stipulation that the water is "up for grabs." The point is that there is no objective description of the situation independent of normative assumptions. Thus, in R. 'Akiva's view, the water is simply unavailable for rescuing the other person; hence failing to save him constitutes no breach of duty and involves no culpable omission of letting him die.

In this canteen case, the choice seems to be determined by the situation. Without denying the two travelers' equal "redness of blood," the precious water goes to its rightful owner.[8] The other would, by Rava's very reasoning, be prohibited from forcibly taking the canteen; that would indeed constitute murder.

But what should be done when the situation leaves the choice to be made? Suppose the travelers number three, and only one of them has water—enough, after meeting her own needs, to save but one of her companions. Now her situation resembles that of the physician (or other agent in the health-care system) who must choose whom to rescue. Recalling Rava's dictum, it seems that she must be guided by a principle of equality. Following Childress's suggestion, it might be thought that such equality would be best pursued by flipping a coin.

In fact, it is striking that in the Halakhic tradition recourse to a lottery seems never to be advocated with regard to choosing between lives. It should be noted that the traditional function of lottery is by no means as an instrument of random chance; rather it is employed as a kind of supernatural device, in order to discover who in God's eyes is guilty. In the biblical story of Jonah, for example, the sailors cast lots to identify the person who was the object of God's wrath and therefore a danger to the entire ship. Through this device, Jonah was properly identified as the culprit and eventually, upon his own insistence, thrown overboard.

For the Jewish theistic tradition, turning to divine selection by lottery could conceivably have been a serious option.[9] The consistent avoidance of such a solution here implies a clear separation between the divine and human domains, consistent with the Maimonidean approach of Part I. Above and beyond human control, it is God who determines the final outcome of medical efforts, but within the scope of human action, human agents must shoulder the responsibility. Rather than second-guess divine judgment, they must contend directly with the various persons seeking to be rescued.

To further explore this approach, let us now turn to a contemporary Halakhic advocacy of rational choice, which comes coupled with a non-random rationale for the Queue Principle.

IV. Queue and Commitment

The position we shall examine seems to be commonly shared by contemporary Halakhic writers; I quote here a short discourse by one of its most lucid explicators, M. Feinstein.

Lasting Life Versus Temporary Life—
Who Takes Precedence?

Regarding two patients: one, in the doctors' estimate, can be treated only toward temporary life, i.e., they have some ability to prolong his life; sometimes all they can do is relieve his suffering, yet this requires intensive care. The other can, in their estimate, be cured, but they do not [at the outset] know whether he will require the intensive care provided in that ward. Now the ward has only one bed; so who takes precedence for admittance to the intensive care [ward]—

a) initially, if they arrive simultaneously, or
b) after the fact, if [at first] one only had arrived and they admitted him, but—before his treatment had begun—the other arrived.—?

It seems to me that if they both arrive simultaneously—that is, as long as neither has been admitted— he ought to be admitted first who, in the view of the doctors there present, can be cured, if his treatment too must begin immediately. [This is to be done] if necessary, even without certainty [as to whether he will in fact require intensive care]. But if they have already admitted the patient who, in their opinion, can only be granted temporary life, they may not remove him from there. [This holds] not only if they rightly admitted him, because the other patient had not yet been present, but even if they acted wrongly (whether by error or deliberately): they may not remove him from there.

The reason for this is simple. Certainly, the life of he who can be cured and live out his expected average life span, takes precedence over that of one who is about to die of his illness, where the doctors know of no cure to this illness. This, however, relates only to third parties, as the patient himself has no duty to rescue others at the cost of his life. Thus once he has been admitted into the ward to be treated, he has become entitled to his place. This is true not only when he is paying for his stay at the hospital, but even when he is not paying—whether because they (generally) extend treatment without charge, or (even) because they do so only for the poor, and he is poor. In any case, by virtue of being brought there, he has acquired the time he needs to be there, and the obligations which lie upon the hospital and the doctors therein to heal him. He [for his part,] has no duty— and is even, perhaps, forbidden—to give over his entitlement, through which he will live his temporary life, i.e., the short time he might live, to another patient, even such as can live, once cured, all his appointed days.

It stands to reason that even if the second patient, who can be cured, is also now in critical condition, which would [definitely] call for immediate admission to the ward—still they may not remove the first one who is already there, even though his life is, in their estimate, only temporary life. For that patient has no duty to rescue, at the cost of his life, even from certain death. It is only before they have admitted the patient who can only be treated toward temporary life, that they should first admit the [other] imperiled patient who ought to be treated first, despite having arrived later.[10]

Feinstein's striking assertion that a significantly higher life expectancy should be reason for granting priority is surely debatable and shall be discussed below. Yet no less striking is his contrast between the two situations, before and after the first patient is admitted. The crucial idea is expressed in his statement, that "once he has been admitted into the ward to be treated, he has become entitled to his place." Feinstein emphasizes that this entitlement has nothing to do with financial acquisition of medical services. As he puts it, there are two objects for this acquisition: "he has acquired the time he needs to be there, and the obligations which lie upon the hospital and the doctors therein to heal him." Clearly, the crucial entitlement for the patient is to the individual and institutional "obligations to heal him." What may seem problematic, however, is the notion that the physicians' moral duties can become the entitlement of one patient to the exclusion of another, even trumping the proper priority.

If it is assumed that we have a general, uncapped duty to save all endangered people, this problem seems virtually intractable. Positing such a general duty amounts to recognizing a broad set of individual duties toward the numerous endangered persons within our potential reach. At any given moment, there are many more such people than we can actually save, so we are continually faced with a multiple conflict of duties. Suppose these can be ranked, on some grounds, each being assigned a relative priority.[11] In principle, this should decide all potential conflicts in advance. In any actual conflict, then, we should act in accordance with the appropriate ranking, regardless of the happenstance sequence of our encounters.

In contrast to this, Feinstein's position implicitly depends on an alternative approach akin to R. 'Akiva's view, as expounded in the previous section. This approach emphasizes that our duties cannot exceed our capabilities, and therefore denies that we have a general duty to save all endangered persons. Instead, we have a concrete, capacity-bound duty to rescue the endangered individual we encounter.[12] The encounter thus commits us to that person, and if that commitment exhausts our capability, we have no further duty to (impossibly) save yet other people.

The commitment which the staff makes to the patient in admitting him to the ward furnishes the basis for his "entitlement." Now that they have a concrete duty to rescue him, letting him die would constitute a culpable omission tantamount to killing. They are therefore forbidden from terminating his treatment in order to save another.

Only when the two prospective patients arrive "simultaneously" is there room for a principled choice. As Feinstein defines this situation, both are present, but neither has yet been admitted. Here, choosing to admit the one does not involve a breach of duty toward the other. The duty to save lives to the extent of one's capacity simply requires that some one patient be admitted; the commitment to either of them, once established, will be equally binding. Meanwhile, in choosing the one to whom they should make their commitment, the intensive care staff rightly compare the prospects of both candidate patients. In this, Feinstein is quite willing to endorse consequentialist considerations.

Like any criteria employed in such choices, these considerations do, however, require justification. Even if the staff, in choosing to admit one patient, are in no way guilty of letting the other die, the basis for their actual choice, such as a differential in life-expectancy, is still subject to criticism. If each human being is made uniquely in God's image, how can human lives be ranked or assessed in quantitative terms? In the final sections of this chapter, I shall focus on the issue of quantitative considerations in health care, viewed from the perspective of an individual agent.[13]

V. Counting Lives

Is Feinstein, in giving preference to the life of the patient with a greater life-expectancy, departing from Rava's principle of equality? Clearly, any qualitative consideration ought to be inadmissible; each person's blood is "equally red." But are more "life-years"—or, for that matter, more lives—more valuable than fewer ones? In the Halakhic tradition, this issue came to be discussed in the context of threats to life posed by human agency, rather than by illness, as in the medical setting:

> . . . If a group is told by heathens:
> Hand over one of your number and we shall kill him;
> otherwise, we shall kill all of you!
> — they should all be killed,
> rather than surrender one individual of Israel.

> (MT, "Foundations of the Torah" 5:5)

This position has a complex history in talmudic law which need not concern us here directly, although it is essential for a full appreciation of Maimonides's ruling. One important distinction, however, relates to designating the individual who might be handed over; our discussion here will proceed on the presumption that the heathens' demand specifies a particular person. For our current purpose, let us posit further that the determining factor in this ruling is not the confrontation with the "heathens," but rather a general pronouncement, according to which no individual may be sacrificed for the sake of the many.

Is such a ruling consistent with the commitment, reflected in Rava's principle, to the basic equality of persons? Does not basic equality rather imply the opposite, that many lives are more valuable than one? This criticism, first expressed by *Ramakh*[14] (Provence, twelfth century), is quoted in the classical commentary on Maimonides's code by R. Joseph Caro (Israel, sixteenth century), who then proceeds to offer a defense of Maimonides's ruling:

Ramakh writes:

> "I know not the reason for this. For the Talmud grounds the requirement (with regard to bloodshed) to be killed rather than transgress, in the reason 'Who is to say that your blood is redder—perhaps his blood is redder?'
>
> Now here this reason does not apply, for they all stand to be killed as well as that individual himself; it is therefore better that he alone be killed and they all be spared!"

—possibly, his [=Maimonides'] view is this: that the reason offered as grounds for the requirement to be killed rather than commit bloodshed, is not the main basis for that rule. Rather, they [=the sages] had a tradition to that effect. They grounded the rule in reason as far as that would go, but in fact, even where this reason is not applicable—the rule is the same: one should be killed rather than transgress. (*Keseph Mishneh* ad loc)

By *Ramakh*'s reading, there is a consequentialist tendency latent in Rava's argument, with its focus on the two alternative deaths. The rhetorical question about redness of blood might be paraphrased, "Seeing that either course of action will result in a death, how can you presume to judge the one outcome less undesirable than the other?" It is the very equality of one life to (any) one other life which makes this reason compelling, but by the same token, disparity between outcomes should make a crucial difference.

In order to justify Maimonides's ruling, Caro is prepared to postulate that the talmudic sages were (at least in this instance) committed more to the received law than to the argument in which they say it is grounded. After all, the positive legal tradition antedates the proffered explanation; the original law, we are asked to assume, was deontological, categorically forbidding bloodshed whatever the consequences.

A radical moral demand similar to Maimonides's ruling was set forth in modern times by E. Cahn with reference to the trial of seaman Holmes in Philadelphia in 1842. Holmes had been in an overcrowded, endangered lifeboat along with other crewmen and more than thirty passengers, and had taken part in casting several passengers into the sea; he was convicted of "unlawful homicide." After raising the (unrealized) possibility of some people volunteering to go overboard, Cahn (1955, p. 71) writes:

> I am driven to conclude that otherwise—that is, if none sacrifice themselves of free will to spare the others— they must all wait and die together . . . no one can survive intact by means of the killing.

Siding with Holmes's judge, most contemporary writers disagree with Cahn's conclusion, despite sharing his commitment to the equality of persons. Like *Ramakh*, they judge it better that only one (or some) should die rather than all; the quantitative difference is morally significant.

Ramakh himself seems to support only a borderline case of preferring the many, since he emphasizes that the specified individual would be doomed in any eventuality. But other thinkers, including earlier rabbis and contemporary philosophers, advocate going beyond that, sacrificing the one so as to save a community. Following through on the logic of *Ramakh*'s argument, they would extend it also to a case where the prospective victim is initially safe. For is not the blood of many "redder" than the blood of one?

This view is most readily understandable from a political perspective, wherein the heathens are conceived as, say, surrounding a town.[15] Political decision making notoriously involves incurring "dirty hands," which often means being prepared to sacrifice some for the many. A prime example of this pertains to the fate of soldiers conscripted and sent forth to risk death for the sake of community survival.[16]

Should this approach be applied also to medical decision making? Few indeed seem willing to endorse the "survival lottery" discussed by Harris (1975), namely, random selection of an individual to be cut up in order to save—by transplanting his or her various organs—several persons from impending death.[17] Indeed, the practices of medicine and of politics appear, at least in this context, to be diametrically opposed; medicine is widely perceived as the epitome of a moral commitment to the individual.

Between these two poles, there are many social settings which might raise questions of "counting lives." An intricate array of problem cases has been extensively discussed in philosophical literature. One classical cluster has been dubbed "trolley problems," which pose various choices involving diverting or obstructing a runaway trolley so as to reduce the number of lives lost.[18] It may well be that some of the moral judgments analyzed in these discussions are best understood as answers to the question: to what extent might an agent such as a trolley driver have 'public responsibilities' similar to those of persons in political office?

In the context of medical practice, however, proposals such as the "survival lottery" are definitely excluded, and rightly so. It is impermissible to kill one patient or (by withdrawing treatment) to let him or her die, in order to save several patients.[19] The crucial problem is not how to justify this deontological commitment, but rather how to explain why the very same reason should not apply to decisions about whom to rescue. If I decide to sail west to rescue five people, rather than sailing east to rescue one person, am I not thereby breaching the commitment to the value of a single life? Can I justify myself by saying, "But I had to save the five," without implying by the same token a justification of the "survival lottery?"

Taurek (1977) has indeed argued that an outright decision to sail west would in fact constitute an unjustified counting of lives. Unlike Cahn's prescription disallowing the casting of any individuals overboard to the effect that "they must all wait and die together," Taurek proposes that the rescuer ought to decide whither to sail by the toss of a coin. Sharing Taurek's rejection of an outright preference for the many, F.M. Kamm (1985) has proposed a more modest solution employing a six-sided die; the lone person is thereby given one chance in six. Kamm argues convincingly that such a procedure more properly constitutes equal treatment of each individual.

I believe that these positions are only plausible under the "general duty" conception depicted in the previous section. If one is in principle obligated to rescue all claimants, failing to save any individual becomes tantamount to *sacrificing* him or her. Kamm says, for example, that a certain implication of treating people as equals ". . . is something we simply *owe* each individual."[20] Choosing whom not to rescue is therefore not dissimilar to choosing whom to kill, and as it is wrong to kill one in order to save many, it is prohibited to prefer saving many over saving a single person.

Under the alternative conception of "concrete duty," however, an outright decision to sail west makes perfect sense. Beyond the agent's capacity, there is no duty toward the person who remains unrescued, and that person is thus not being sacrificed to save the many to whom the resources are rightly committed.

Clearly, Feinstein extends this same reasoning to a quantitative weighing of "life-years," at least where there is a substantial difference in expected outcome. No person may be terminated in order to save someone with a greater life-expectancy or, for that matter, in order to save many people. But, despite the basic equality of people, such quantitative considerations are legitimate in choosing to whom resources should be committed.

VI. Deliberate Choice: Further Possibilities

Feinstein's position, as explicated above, is representative of Halakhic approaches to the duties of lifesaving. Some cases of withdrawing aid fall, like outright killing, under the deontological prohibition of bloodshed; they are clearly distinguished from cases where no commitment has yet been made. In the latter sort of cases, the proper question is not "whom to sacrifice" but "whom to rescue."

In response to this question, it is possible (going beyond Feinstein) to propose other criteria for deliberate choice while accepting that any concrete duty, once defined, supersedes all such criteria. Any grounds proposed for deliberate choice must, of course, be critically examined; if it is concluded that they are unacceptable, the egalitarian system of deciding by lot should be preferred.

Let us examine, then, a poignant view on deliberate choice from the Halakhic tradition. The textual foundation for this view is found in the Mishna's discussion of precedence amongst objects and persons with regard to temporal sequence in temple ritual. At the end of this discussion, the Mishna adds this general statement (*horayot* 3:8):

1. A Kohen takes precedence over a Levite, a Levite over an Israelite, an Israelite over a *mamzer* . . .[21]

2. When is this so? When they are all equal. But if the *mamzer* is a scholar and the High Priest an ignoramus—the *mamzer* scholar takes precedence over the ignorant High Priest.

This text seems clearly comprised of two strata, and I have taken the liberty of marking them as clauses 1 and 2. The first clause defines a system of class hierarchy based on lineage. Superimposed upon this is the revolutionary final clause; decisive priority is given to acquired status attained through individual achievement. It seems plausible to assume here not simply a dual division of "scholar" versus "ignoramus," but rather a range of subtle differences in learning. Therefore, cases in which both persons are "equal" will be quite rare; differences of accomplishment will generally override class origin.

What are the purposes for which these pronouncements of precedence are intended? Another Mishnaic statement (*gittin* 5:8) suggests a context of social honors, such as the synagogue ritual in which individuals are called for reading the Torah; a Kohen should be called up first. But a mainstream traditional reading accords these rules of precedence a quite sweeping scope, applying them to choices in saving lives.[22] M. Herschler embraces this reading of the Mishnaic "order of precedence" but makes it subservient to the priority-by-expected-outcome already familiar from Feinstein's discussion:

> If there is only one machine in the hospital and there are several patients who need it, and all of them are equal in terms of illness and danger—one should follow the order of precedence defined in the Mishna.[23]

Herschler also insists that the Mishnaic order of precedence could never, of course, justify either killing or terminating care of a person of lower class in order to save a Kohen or a scholar. Indeed, priorities based upon status are conceptually excluded, in his view, from ascribing relative values to human lives. They are only to be invoked as a last-resort alternative to arbitrariness:

> . . . the precedence given the Kohen is not based on essential valuation, for "Who is to say [that your blood is redder]?!" Rather, since [the rescuer] must make an arbitrary choice, he ought to fulfill the commandment of honoring the Kohen.[24]

An apparently similar distinction, widespread in Western culture, relates to the preference traditionally given to women and children. Certainly, chivalry in its age did not prescribe that any man be killed in order to save a woman or a child. But when a choice had to be made, it seemed right to honor the rules of chivalry rather than choose arbitrarily.

A comparable approach is espoused by J. Babad (Poland, nineteenth century), who holds that if the "two walking in the desert" are an adult and a child, then ". . . certainly [the adult] is required to give [the water] to save the child, though he himself will die."[25] His reason for this is, however, cast in terms of specific obligations, rather in the spirit of Feinstein's analysis. Babad argues that the basic dilemma (emphasized radically by Ben-Patura; see section III above) is due to the mutual obligations of rescue pertaining between two adults. Since a child is, however, legally exempt from all Halakhic obligations, there remains a clear and unilateral obligation upon the adult to save it. It follows that a third-party rescuer must equally give precedence to the child, since if the water were given to the adult he or she would in any case be obliged to save the child instead.

Perhaps the best account of chivalrous priorities would proceed in analogous manner, emphasizing men's duty to protect the powerless. In modern society this would surely not extend to women. Following Babad's approach, it may be similarly asserted that a woman and a man, trapped in the desert, have equal mutual obligations of rescue; the same plainly extends to a priest and a layman. These obligations ought to establish a principle of equality in lifesaving over and above any class distinctions.

Indeed, even in terms of the Mishnaic tradition itself, it seems doubtful that class distinctions ought to be invoked at all in contemporary settings. According to the Mishna mentioned above (*gittin* 5:8), the preference given to the priest in everyday contexts of social respect is rooted in "the ways of peace." In a class-oriented society, following the accepted groove of social status and honors may arguably serve to reduce social friction. But in a modern democratic society, "ways of peace" require rather eschewal of all traces of honors and preferences based upon status. E. Rackman (1986, at 241–42), in fact, firmly rejects the application of the Mishnaic "order of precedence" to issues of lifesaving.[26] It is also noteworthy that Feinstein himself significantly omits all mention of both the original precedence by lineage and the superimposed priority of scholars.

This position seems most consistent with the initial principle of our discussion: the conviction that all human beings are created in the image of God. Deliberate choice may be employed, at most, on the basis of expected medical outcomes and life-expectancy ("temporary life vs. lasting life"). Considerations that look, however, to any personal attributes should be simply ruled out. In choosing between patients with similar prognoses, arbitrary choice has great positive value. It seems right, then, to cast lots, not as a vehicle for divine selection, but as the only means of selection that is (in the words of Holmes's judge) consistent with "humanity and justice." Casting lots concretizes the arbitrary nature of the cruel choice and thereby clearly symbolizes the substantive equality among all people created in the image of God.

Notes

1. For a classical analysis, see Williams (1971).

2. BT *sanhedrin* 74a, emphasis added.

3. See the concluding section on Deliberate Choice below.

4. Childress (1983), at 648. See similarly Ramsey (1970) Ch. 7: "Choosing How To Choose: Patients and Sparse Medical Resources" (pp. 239–75).

5. This seems to concede that *in principle* judgment of desert is possible, merely denying human capability to determine it. In terms of the talmudic metaphor, the blood of some may be redder, but they cannot with confidence be identified. The extent to which a human agent, resorting to chance, will approximate the ideal choice, is of course a matter of luck—a kind of "moral luck" [an idea discussed in some detail by B. Williams and T. Nagel, and applied to medical ethics by D. Dickenson (1991)]

6. E.g., by Dr. G.E. Schreiner, quoted by Childress (ibid) at 644.

7. I employ here this ambiguous term advisedly. I mention explicitly a suggestion of removing a respirator, which in the context of euthanasia occupies a kind of middle position between active and passive measures. But the same question may arise with respect to unambiguous, outright killing. This is approached when we are urged to adopt criteria of "brain death" partly on the grounds that this facilitates removal of organs for transplanta-

tions; we are to abandon the doomed patient—declare him dead—in order to rescue someone else.

This whole line of criticism might be answered easily by those who readily accept the moral significance of the active/passive distinction. But having argued to deny this significance in the context of euthanasia, I must deal seriously with the accusation of inconsistency (see sections III and V below).

8. The detail is, however, rather scarce; we might wish to inquire how it came to pass that only one has a canteen in his hand. Was he more enterprising in finding a meager supply in the wilderness, or perhaps more prudent in carrying an adequate quantity in the first place? Or was he more able, by the luck of stronger constitution, to carry a canteen to this critical point? And also, what is the relationship between the two travellers—have they made any prior promises or commitments to each other? Is this perhaps their shared canteen which, at the moment they discover they have lost their way, happens to be in the hands of the one? Questions of this sort are crucial for dealing in depth with the moral fable, and even more so for dealing with the real-life corollary of R. 'Akiva's position, which seems to endow ownership (or possession) of resources with striking moral authority.

9. For an interesting discussion, see *Responsa Havot Ya'ir* (Rabbi Ya'ir Bakhrakh, Frankfurt, 1699) section 61.

10. This discourse was published in the yearbook *Techumin* Vol. 5 (Tsomet: Alon Shevut, 1984; Hebrew), pp. 214–15. Feinstein concludes with this practical qualification:

All this, however, applies only in such a manner wherein the [first] imperiled patient will not realize that in the doctors' estimate he cannot be cured. For if through this [i.e., through seeing the other admitted first] he will realize that he cannot be cured, there is room for concern lest his death be hastened and his mind be set in turmoil—which is definitely forbidden. Now since most commonly he does not realize his condition (for they take care not to inform him, and are indeed forbidden to inform him) he who arrived first should be admitted first. In fact, even if the patient realizes his condition, there is room for concern lest his mind be set in turmoil, for he will think that they are already considering him a nonentity, as they are taking no care of him. Therefore in practice it seems unlikely that the first one's condition would not deteriorate when they admit the other ahead of him. Thus they should admit first whoever came first, even if it is the patient whom they believe incurable. They ought, however, to find a way so that the other as well should not go without the necessary treatment, even at some other place—if possible.

11. If they cannot be ranked, we can either adopt ben-Patura's approach and save no one, or follow Childress and employ a lottery.

12. A roughly similar distinction is put forward by Judith Lichtenberg in the course of a different, though related, discussion; cf. Lichtenberg (1982) at 214.

13. At this stage, we shall follow Feinstein in focusing exclusively on such an individual perspective. But even before engaging (in Chapter 6) in an examination from the public perspective, I must emphasize the deficiency of sticking to the individual perspective alone. Feinstein's mode of discourse leaves no room for the moral perspective of other employees of the hospital—those entrusted with long-range planning or with formulating its institutional relationship with the community at large. Even granting that individual physicians are bound only (or chiefly) by the particular obligations they incur vis-a-vis their actual patients, it seems inconceivable that the same can be true of the hospital. Even less can this perspective be carried over to the level of social planning and administration, which is the locus of much of the decision making regarding choices of life and death.

In order to properly address these broader issues of public policy, we shall have to wait until we have studied the classical Halakhic discussion of long-range policy in health care, formulated in the context of the conflict between medical research and respect for the dead. In the present context, we must still examine Feinstein's bold assertion regarding the relevance of life expectancy.

14. Rabbi Moshe ha-Kohen of Lunel.

15. Quite possibly, this may have been the original context of the discussion recorded in Tosefta *terumot* 7:20; see Daube (1965).

16. The special character of politics as involving trespassing boundaries of common morality has been discussed in modern

times by Max Weber [see his "Politics as a Vocation," in *From Max Weber: Essays in Sociology* (transl. & ed. by H.H. Gerth & C.W. Mills, NY, 1946), pp. 77–128]. Subsequently, following the name of a play by Sartre, this came to be called "The Problem of Dirty Hands"; see Walzer (1973).

17. See Leiman (1983).

18. The literature on "trolley problems" harks back to Philipa Foot's essay, "The Problem of Abortion and the Doctrine of Double Effect" (1967), reprinted in Steinbock & Norcross (1994), pp. 266–79. Some doubts about the permission, assumed by Foot and others, to sacrifice "innocent bystanders," has been expressed lately be Jeff McMahan (1994). In the context of individual morality, as opposed to political or collective morality, I think these doubts are well-founded; see Zohar (1993b).

19. For a detailed discussion, see McMahan (1993).

20. The context of this statement is very specific, but it is characteristic of Kamm's argument throughout. I do not mean to say that Kamm herself equates killing with letting die, nor that Taurek does; on the contrary, they both make it abundantly clear that they do not. In fact, Taurek's fundamental approach is not very distant from that expounded below. But still, I think Taurek's prime recommendation is most plausible from the "general duty" perspective.

21. For an explanation of this term, see above Chapter 3, section II.

22. Bet Yosef, YD 251, and *rema*, YD 252:8. For further references and analysis, see Dikhovsky (1976).

23. Herschler (1981) at 40.

24. For a similar emphasis, see Dikhovsky (1976) at 64.

25. Minhat Hinukh, Lemberg (1869) Mitzvah 296.

26. Support for this interpretation is found in an immediately preceding Mishnaic clause, which can be translated as "A man takes precedence over a woman for sustenance, while a woman takes precedence over a man for clothing," etc. According to this reading, the gender difference involves distinctive needs, and with regard to life itself, everyone's need is, of course, identical.

5

Human Bodies: Long-Term Benefits and Symbolic Constraints

I. Normative Constraints on Using the Dead

From the perspective of medical practice and research, the human body might be viewed as a valuable resource. Living persons, however, are rightly protected from medically cannibalistic designs; this protection was a major theme of our discussion in the previous chapter. But when the person is gone, it arguably becomes plausible to regard the remaining cadaver as a resource for helping others.

Dead bodies, in being dissected, can be a source of knowledge both for medical science in general and for individual students training for medical practice. In addition, particular bodies, through post-mortems, can be sources of more specific knowledge regarding various pathologies and treatments. And finally, body organs can be used directly for transplantation into needy patients. But despite the evident benefits of these uses, cadavers are not simply up for grabs; moral and legal norms strictly constrain their utilization for even medical purposes.

In limiting the use of cadavers, what interests precisely do these norms aim to protect? In the United States, the Uniform Anatomical Gift Act governs the use of human bodies (or their parts) not merely for research, but primarily for the newer purposes of transplantation. It recognizes the right of the individual to determine whether her or his body shall be made available for various medical uses.[1] As D. Meyers (1990, at 186) explains the purpose of a change in, for example, Massachusetts law, it was so that "[t]he person should be able to decide what will be done with his body after death, unless public interest, not merely preference of relatives, requires otherwise."

This rationale differs from that found in the Halakhic tradition, which centers here less on the wishes of the dead or of their family than on the inviolability of a human cadaver as such. The Halakhic prohibition of "disfiguring the dead" is linked to the biblical law which forbids exposure of an executed criminal's body, demanding instead burial "that same day" (Deut. 21:22–23). From this radical case the Rabbis plausibly generalized an injunction against "anyone who leaves his dead [relative unburied] overnight" (Mishna, *sanhedrin* 6:5). The reason for this ruling is illuminated in a parable; as in the parables we examined above, God is represented by a king:

> Two brothers, identical twins,
> [lived] in the same city.
> One was appointed king,
>   while the other became a highwayman;
> the king ordered him hanged.
> Everyone who saw him exclaimed:
>   "The king is hanged!"
> The king ordered him taken down.
>
> (BT *sanhedrin* 46b)

The description of "identical twins" clearly draws on the belief that humans are made "in God's image." As we saw in the opening section of Part II, the severity of murder was emphasized by describing it as diminishing the divine image. The Twins Parable extends the notion to the dead human body; it too bears the same resemblance.

True, prompt and respectful burial is seen also as an act of lovingkindness toward the deceased.[2] But failure in the duty of burial, or infraction of the concomitant injunction against disfiguring the dead, is seen by some Halakhic writers also as a violation of the human person as divine symbol,[3] distinct from any harm to the interests of this particular individual.

The Halakhic and Western traditions thus share a view of the human cadaver as significantly related to the person; human remains are not simply flesh and bones. Utilizing them for medical purposes is therefore normatively different from using non-human substances and materials; it requires justification in terms of its purpose—commonly, the saving of lives. But this gives rise to a knotty problem: why should the protection of cadavers, whatever its value-basis, not be superseded by the necessity of saving lives?

Perhaps the best way to emphasize this problem is through considering a case which occurred in Israel in 1983.[4] A prominent kidney-transplant surgeon was accused of violating the Israeli equivalent of the Anatomical Gift Act. There was little dispute over the facts; the defendant had taken a kidney from a cadaver without making sufficient effort, as required by law, to first notify the deceased's next-of-kin.

A noteworthy, though not, perhaps, surprising, aspect of the defense was that it at no point tried to justify the surgeon by referring to the *purpose* of his action, namely, saving the life of his patient. In legal terms, that would have meant putting forward the defense of "necessity." This defense consists in claiming that the defendant ought to have broken a particular law, although the law protects against a definite harm, in order to prevent a far more grievous harm. According to prevalent legal theory, the necessity defense goes beyond a mere excuse. It does not, that is, seek merely to reduce the defendant's culpability for an act acknowledged to be objectively wrong. Rather, it seeks to establish that the act itself was the best under the given circumstances.[5]

Where the necessity defense is valid, it therefore implies not only a shield from legal punishment, but also a moral justification. It rests on recognizing a clash between two values: the one protected by the law versus the greater value (standardly, saving life or limb) secured by the act under consideration.

Had the necessity defense been tried, should the judge have accepted it? Or, in more explicit moral terms, what should we tell the surgeon to do if he turns to us in advance seeking moral counsel?[6] Does not the value of the life-saving transplantation outweigh any concerns, however real and important they may be, which find expression in the law protecting cadavers?

Halakhically, this question would be put in terms of conflicting duties. The surgeon, like any other person, has a duty of respect toward the dead body but also a duty to save lives, and traditionally, life saving takes precedence over any other "commandment" (save three: the prohibitions of bloodshed, idolatry, and incest[7]). Halakhic counsel to the surgeon's hypothetical query would thus seem to converge with the reasoning behind the necessity defense.

If this reasoning is accepted, medical practice, insofar as it constitutes life-saving, should be granted a rather sweeping mandate to override most ordinary norms and constraints. This ought to apply, it seems, not only to disrespect for cadavers but also, for example, to lying and stealing. The paradigm for this would be the ambulance driver, who is not only allowed but actually expected to speed through red lights, drive on the wrong side of the road, across people's lawns, etc. Traffic rules and trespass laws have their value, but in an emergency they are superseded by the greater value of saving a life.

What is the proper scope for applying this paradigm? Not only medical practice but also medical research labors toward the saving of lives. Does this confer the privileged status of "life-saving" upon all the activities carried out in these fields? The question can be put also in terms of the relation between ends and means. To what extent can the overall end of saving lives justify the means employed in its pursuit?

This question, which has general significance for several realms of social ethics, has been the subject of an intense Halakhic debate focused specifically on medical utilization of cadavers. The following sections trace that debate across two hundred years. Analysis of the rival positions will reveal not only their differences, but also a shared orientation toward the centrality of *obligation* in

normative discourse. In the context of long-range, cooperative projects like medical research, this orientation is
shown to involve serious difficulties. In the final section, I
seek to address these difficulties in terms of the contemporary philosophical discussion of Role Morality.

II. Defining 'Emergency': "A Patient Before Us"

In the second part of the eighteenth century, London
was the locus of new efforts in surgery. Initial success was
not great, and surgeons obviously wished to conduct
autopsies in order to improve their technique.[8] A Halakhic
question about this was referred to one of the leading
Halakhists of the day, Rabbi Yehezqel Landa of Prague;
Landa responded:

> Concerning your treatise which you sent me, in which
> you discuss the question you received from the holy
> community of London, regarding a case that occurred
> there.

> —A person fell ill with the affliction of a stone in his
> bladder, and the surgeons cut in their accustomed
> manner of healing such an affliction, and he was not
> healed but died.[9] Now the local rabbis were asked
> whether it is permitted to cut into the dead [person]'s
> body in that place in order to see directly the source of
> this affliction, so as to gain from it knowledge regard-
> ing the surgeons' future conduct, should such a case
> occur [again]; so that they would know how to con-
> duct themselves with respect to the cutting necessary
> for healing, and not cut excessively, so as to minimize
> the dangers of cutting. Is it forbidden because it
> involves disfigurement and disrespect of this deceased
> person, or is it permitted because it might bring about
> saving of life in the future, through becoming thor-
> oughly proficient in this art?

The London rabbis had been divided on the issue.[10] After
some detailed discussion of the arguments on both sides,

which had focused chiefly on ancient precedents, but also on some analysis of just what constitutes "disfigurement," the author presses his main point. It is made against the backdrop of the classical Halakhic statement about the precedence of life-saving, which is stated in the *Mishna* with respect to the severe ritual prohibitions of Shabbat observance:[11]

> —But I am perplexed: if this is to be considered even an "uncertain saving of life," what need have you of all this *pilpul* [=hairsplitting casuistry]? Is the law not clearly set down, that even an uncertainty causes the Shabbat prohibitions to be suspended?!

> —However, all this only applies when there is an uncertain mortal risk **before us**[12] (*lefaneynu*) . . . while in our case there is no patient here who needs this, but rather they merely wish to acquire this knowledge lest perhaps a patient should turn up who needs it. Certainly we do not, on account of this slight chance, suspend any prohibition . . . For if you define such a slight chance as "uncertain [saving of] life," then all medical work, production of medications and preparation of scalpels for bloodletting would be permitted on Shabbat, lest today or tonight a patient requiring them should turn up . . .

> No one should dare permit this; and even the gentile physicians do not experiment in the skills of surgery on any dead, except those executed or those who personally agreed to it while alive.[13] And if we—spare us!— are lenient in this issue, then all the dead will be dissected in order to learn the arrangement and nature of the inner organs so as to know how to heal the living. (*Noda Bihuda* II, YD 210)

Landa does not entertain the possibility that such a dissection might be defined by virtue of its purpose as involving no disrespect for the dead. Hence for him the problem is not specific to autopsy, but is rather a general one relating to all potential conflicts between medical research and injunctions reflecting various values. And his position consists in strictly curtailing the scope of 'life-saving'; this concept only applies, he proclaims, to situations with a "patient before us"—in contemporary legal terms, to a "present danger."

It is worth noting an ambiguity in Landa's definition of this crucial condition. On the one hand, it contrasts present with future: "there is no patient *here* who needs this." On the other hand, it emphasizes the low probability of the life-saving result: "we do not, on account of this *slight chance*, suspend any prohibition."

Around the middle of the twentieth century, two prominent Halakhists took up the "before us" requirement. I. Karelitz, basically upholding it, struggled with the inherent ambiguity:

> What makes the difference is not whether there is [a patient] before us or not, but whether it is a present issue.[14] For a situation as would warrant Sounding an Alarm on account of an epidemic (even without a patient before us at the moment), is analogous to enemies who have set siege upon a town near the border (cf. BT *'eruvin* 45a, *ta'anit* 21b);
>
> > [This present danger justifies engaging in active military preparations in neighboring towns, including— if necessary—suspending the Shabbat prohibitions.]
>
> Nevertheless, in peacetime we do not consider [such preparations] to be life-saving, despite the fact that they are likely to be needed at some time or another. Similarly, we do not manufacture weapons on Shabbat in peacetime—for otherwise all the commandments would be canceled.
>
> Rather, "uncertain life-saving" does not include future events of which there is no sign in the present. Indeed, we have no expert knowledge[15] of future things; sometimes what they calculate to be rescue turns out to

be disastrous. Therefore, no judgment should be based
on things far in the future . . . (*Hazon Ish, ohalot*
22:32)

The simple equation of 'far in the future' with 'unknow-
able' appears quite at odds both with the achievements of
modern medicine and with their theoretical underpinnings.
After all, the notion of probabilistic knowledge is central to
statistical analysis of pathological findings. In the next section, we shall see an argument by B.H. 'Uziel against the
entire "before us" attempt at line drawing. But first, it is
important to note Karelitz's fundamental argument for the
very necessity of drawing some line: "Similarly, we do not
manufacture weapons on Shabbat in peacetime—for otherwise all the commandments would be canceled." At first
glance, this concern seems fantastic; how and why would
"*all* the commandments" come to be canceled? Yet upon
reflection, the point appears to be well taken. For let us
suppose that no line is drawn, and the Halakhic rule that
"life saving takes precedence over all the commandments"
is extended to include all activities and enterprises that
are likely to save (some) lives in the long run. Would this
not result in no time or resources ever being available for
other pursuits? Or in non-Halakhic terms, would not such
an expansion of the notion of emergency result in no normative constraints ever having effect in the face of consequentialist considerations?

We shall return to this point when discussing the most
modern—and most radical—drawing of the line by M. Feinstein. But first, let us see the radically opposite argument
of B.H. 'Uziel.

III. Radical Alternatives: 'Uziel and Feinstein

'Uziel starts by quoting Landa's original ruling, and
then continues:

Now as to his claim that there is no patient before us,
but merely [the possibility] lest one turns up, I say:

can a common reality be denied? Certainly there always are more than a few persons afflicted with that same disease; and if he [i.e, the beneficiary] is at the moment unknown to us, tomorrow or [even] today he will become known. This [i.e., conducting a post mortem] is entirely different from producing medications [on Shabbat]—which can be done at any moment or prepared the day before. Here, if the autopsy is not performed on this body due to the prohibition involved, it will never be performed, and this knowledge will remain forever hidden from us, causing the certain death of several persons. (*Mishp'tey 'Uziel* YD 28)

'Uziel clearly recognizes the slim chance of an individual autopsy yielding life-saving knowledge. But he insists that we should rather be considering autopsies cumulatively; what will be the price of a restrictive policy such as that advocated by Landa? If we have reason to predict that without the practice of autopsies fewer lives will be saved, then performing them is to be regarded as "certain saving of life," overriding the relevant prohibitions.[16]

This wide definition of 'life-saving' has far-reaching implications for the moral status of biomedical research. If any practice expected to save some lives in the long run is accorded the supreme status of "life-saving," then are not virtually all realms of biomedical research, theoretical as well as applied, necessarily included? And if so, can it be that pursuit of such research justifies 'suspending' all other pursuits and normative constraints? Are those engaged in such research morally obliged to work incessantly on a constant emergency footing, stealing equipment if necessary—stopping short only of murder? A parallel challenge must be faced in the contemporary Western context, where the bar to autopsies is the requirement of consent. Ought the "necessity" justification be extended in the spirit of 'Uziel's argument, implying, in effect, that operations should proceed unimpeded whether or not consent is granted?

It seems that 'Uziel's logic carries too far, producing an unacceptably inflated notion of 'emergency'. Karelitz's concern must be addressed; "life saving" threatens to engulf everything and some line must be drawn. But, given the proven effects of medical research in general and of postmortem examinations in particular, 'Uziel's critique of the "patient before us" criterion also seems compelling. Is there an alternative way to draw the line?

Feinstein undertakes to meet this challenge by reformulating Landa's initial intuition. He recognizes that, given modern communications, the requirement of "a patient here before us" retains little validity, and also clearly acknowledges the foreseeability of the needs of future patients. Yet he forbids virtually all autopsies,[17] offering a new rationale for this position:

> . . . now concerning dissecting the dead in order to see the source of the affliction so as to acquire knowledge. . . . One has no duty to acquire knowledge of healing. For there is no obligation upon each and every person to acquire the knowledge of medicine in order to heal the sick, present and future; although sick persons are common and the risk is foreseeable. For the obligation by which one is bound is only to rescue his fellow according to his capability. If he is already a physician, there is an obligation upon him to heal his fellows the sick, and if he knows how to swim he is obligated to swim and save a person who is drowning in a river. But a person has no obligation to learn how to swim or how to heal the sick, so that if an opportunity arises for him to rescue or to heal he be capable of rescuing or healing . . .
>
> . . . and thus also dissecting the dead in order to learn from it some [way of] healing—is equally no one's obligation, so that it remains forbidden since it constitutes disfigurement of the dead. (*Iggerot Moshe*, YD II 151)

Feinstein's basic approach here is reminiscent of his doctrine of "concrete duty" which we saw in the previous chapter (section IV). In the present context, he defines the postulate that there is no *obligation* to study medicine. From this premise he argues further that no physician is obligated to expand his life-saving knowledge. 'Ought' implies 'can' in the narrowest sense; no one has any duty beyond his or her present capabilities. In a responsum dated ten years later, Feinstein reaffirmed this basic position (in another context):

> . . . for even were there no physician in the [entire] world, there would be no obligation [under the duty] of life-saving to study medicine. For the duty of life-saving applies to each person according to his capability. If he is a physician, he is obligated to save the sick from their afflictions—but there is no obligation to study medicine in order to save the sick. Just like regarding charity, if one has wealth he is obligated to give charity, but a person has no obligation to engage in business and become rich in order to give charity. (*Iggerot Moshe*, YD III 155)

Unlike Landa and even Karelitz, he recognizes that with respect to the medical endeavor as a whole, patients are ever-present. He thus shares 'Uziel's appreciation of modern medical science as a broad enterprise, yet he differs radically in the assessment of its normative value. For Feinstein, this is restricted by a requirement of immediate presence in another sense, excluding from duties of life saving not future patients but future capabilities.

Regarding the moral status of studying medicine in the first place, this seems strictly correct but somewhat dissatisfying. If the study of medicine is not an "obligation," is it therefore morally neutral, just like the pursuit of wealth? In any case, extending the postulate to those who are already physicians seems extremely strange. What if a physician lacks a specific piece of knowledge possessed by a specialist in the next room—is it not his or her duty to acquire it? And what about reading medical journals, learning newly developed skills, and so on? Feinstein clearly found himself in a bind: if all activities ancillary to the direct saving of life were recognized as life-saving, would not the result be, to quote Karelitz, that "all the commandments would be canceled"? Yet unlike Karelitz, who simply points to this unacceptable implication, Feinstein offers a salient argument which exposes the basic problem of the alternative approach. According to 'Uziel, expected cumulative results can endow a practice with the normative status of life saving. But how precisely does the long-range, collective view transfer to the normative perspective of the individual agent?

When facing the prospect of conducting an autopsy, such an individual is contemplating the direct violation of a prohibition (=disfiguring the dead). What countervailing duty might overcome that prohibition? After all, this particular autopsy, like most others, is likely not to contribute toward the saving of any life, and even if it finally does, its contribution will be infinitesimal. Surely it is wrong to postulate a *duty* to perform such an act, akin to the duty of pulling a drowning person out of a river! And barring such a postulate, what can justify for the individual agent, who is after all the actual locus of moral decision, the violation of clear and important norms?

Both sides to this Halakhic debate seem to share the notion that if it lacks the status of "obligation," acquisition of medical knowledge must yield to any concrete prohibition. For Feinstein, this results in a curious abandonment of social responsibility, while 'Uziel's solution involves an unacceptable inflation of "emergency life-saving." Having traced the Halakhic discussion, we thus end up with an unsettling dichotomy.

The problem seems to inhere in the conceptual paucity of a system in which concrete duty is the sole idiom of normative discourse. In such a system, one imperative can only be overcome by another (superior) imperative.[18] It is this that forces a dichotomous choice between proclaiming an activity "life-saving" on the one hand and denying it any binding value on the other hand. What is missing is a conceptual scheme geared to the workings of a collective, long-range practice. This should make it possible to link the practice's cumulative results to the particular, day-to-day activities of its individual participants. In seeking such a scheme, let us now turn to contemporary discussions of Role Morality.

IV. Role Morality:
The Normative Status of Participation

Not infrequently, the significance of a person's actions derives from her place in a collective enterprise of which she forms a part. Moral assessment of these actions then greatly depends on understanding their function within this wider collaborative scheme. When such a scheme is sustained across time, it becomes an institution, and an individual's function within it comprises her or his role. Justifications for a person's actions through reference to his or her role have been captioned "Role Morality." A careful critical analysis of Role Morality has been offered by D. Luban (1988, 104–47), primarily with respect to the ethics of lawyers' practices. Through presentation and discussion of some of Luban's comments, I will seek in this section to suggest a conceptual approach to judging the duties of individuals in biomedical research.

As long as the demands deriving from one's role are not morally objectionable, one's duty to comply seems rather simple. There is a *contractual* duty toward the institution (or toward its members and officers) to fulfill the role conscientiously. Luban begins his discussion, however, by observing that lawyers are thought to be obligated, by virtue of their role as lawyers, to act in ways which are clearly immoral by any common standard. Within the adversarial system, the role of criminal-defense lawyer is said to require, for example, "to put perjurious clients on the stand, to attempt to discredit opposing witnesses known by [the lawyer] to be telling the truth, even at the cost of humiliating them . . ."[19] It is not simply that such actions are sometimes permitted, but rather that nothing less will do and the lawyer is morally obligated to act in these ways if required by the client's interest. In such instances, a contractual obligation—whether toward the client, the law firm, or the entire institution of the adversary system—can hardly suffice to justify moral transgressions. Are there then other, more compelling grounds for postulating a Role Morality, that is, a view which attributes powerful moral force to role obligations?

Luban points out that in order for such obligations to have any moral force, the institution itself must first of all be justified. It is not enough to refer simply to "my station and its duties"; fulfilling a role within an institution can constitute a moral obligation only if the institution's overall goals are valuable. The value of these goals might then transfer to the duties attached to individual roles, and might thereby yield an argument in favor of following the demands of such roles even in the face of common morality. As a supposedly compelling illustration of Role Morality, Luban asks us to imagine an officer of a famine-relief organization whose role it is to secure trucks for transporting food to a starving village, but who finds that in order to do so she must allow a murder to be committed:

> The officer is in a moral dilemma. Other things being equal, she is under a moral obligation to warn the victim or the police. Let us, at any rate, suppose that it is so. But here, if anywhere, we may wish to permit an institutional excuse. (ibid at 130)

Save for her role in the relief organization, this person would clearly be obligated to warn and rescue the innocent victim. The compelling demands of her role morality, however, supposedly overcome this duty of common morality. But is this truly a convincing example of Role Morality? D. Wueste (1991), commenting on an earlier version of Luban's position, argues that in fact it is simpler to think of this case without any reference to special, role-bound obligations. The agent has no unique duties by virtue of her role as transportation officer in the relief organization. The determining factor lies rather in the circumstances; it is her capacity to save many lives by refraining from saving the one, rather than her institutional role, that (arguably) justifies her action.[20] The role is morally transparent, merely letting through the obligations projected directly by the goals which the institution's members are in a position to serve.

Responding to a similar criticism, Luban indicates a line of response which deserves, in my view, fuller explication. The point is that we must take into account the vast difference in perspective between institutional and individual agency. Luban's example is indeed misleading, since it makes the fate of the starving villagers depend directly and dramatically on the actions of this one officer (although the food itself still must be provided and distributed). More typical of action within institutions are the many mundane activities that go into providing the food, such as preparing mailing lists for soliciting contributions, labelling envelopes, and other tasks.

It is the moral status of activities like these that we have difficulty in weighing against countervailing normative demands, a difficulty spelled out above in the Halakhic dilemma. Taken together these activities are no less essential than the more dramatic activities in the field, yet surely no one would propose that they should similarly take precedence over rescuing a prospective victim from being murdered. Still, they are not morally neutral; the person compiling the mailing list is bound by a moral imperative which is defined by his or her role in the institution and reflects the value of the institution's goals.

This imperative obviously cannot justify killing or letting innocents die "for the sake of the cause," and perhaps—pace Robinhood—it also cannot justify stealing (cf. Dratch, 1990). But I think it may possibly justify lesser transgressions, such as intentional lying aimed at tricking a recalcitrant informant into disclosing a list of potential donors. Where such a justification holds, it will as a rule not make sense from a narrowly individualistic perspective; we need Role Morality because the overall imperative does not apply full-force to each small contribution. The need to get that list, for example, can hardly be construed as "life-saving" (in the Halakhic sense), nor suffice for a plausible "necessity" defense.

The justification, insofar as it is valid, depends on assessing individual actions with reference to the ongoing efforts of the institution. The institution is able to achieve its goals by virtue of the various functions performed within it; the value of those goals is therefore distributed across the particular roles attached to those functions. The duty of an individual person to his or her role thus draws its moral force from the value of the collective goals, mediated by the institutional structure.

The notion of Role Morality thus provides a crucial middle ground between 'Uziel's excessive urgency and Feinstein's denial of responsibility. Feinstein is right to insist on a normative account centered on the individual agent, and to deny that a person working in biomedical research can be simply equated to one engaged in emergency life saving. But 'Uziel is also right to insist that we take into account the cumulative effects of individual actions.

Thus, the unsettling dichotomy of the Halakhic discussion helps us appreciate the significance of explicit reference to institutional goals and to Role Morality. This conceptual scheme explains the moral status of obligations attached to the role of a medical researcher, such as a pathologist performing an autopsy. Although it is not imbued with the full force of life-saving urgency, performing the autopsy is also not morally neutral. If we insist on the language of 'duty', then we must recognize a class of duties derived from people's roles. The role of researcher, then, certainly carries a duty to learn how to heal. This duty may arguably suffice to outweigh considerations of respect for the dead, whether grounded in a conception of God's image or in a concern for the deceased's autonomy.

V. Conclusion: Divine Image—Symbol versus Value

In the opening section of Part II, we examined two distinct interpretations of the doctrine that human beings are made in God's image. One interpretation depicts people mainly as instruments of divine glory; this, I suggested, hardly adds up to religious humanism. The alternative interpretation, in contradistinction, attributes divine value to each human being in himself or herself.

The Halakhic discussion we have followed in this chapter addresses a conflict between opposing implications of these different notions of the divine image. One implication already introduced in Chapter 4 is the supreme imperative of life-saving, which follows from the *divine value* of human life. In the context of autopsies, however, this conflicts with the conception of the human body as *divine symbol*, which implies a requirement of respect for the dead.

The fact that many rabbis hesitate to grant medical research supremacy over respect for the dead does not necessarily signify a prevalent disavowal of religious humanism in favor of divine symbolism. On the contrary, wherever respect for the dead comes into conflict with immediate life saving, it is the latter which takes absolute precedence. The problem lies, rather, in defining the proper scope of the life-saving imperative. The difficulty seems to be that this duty-centered system lacks a conceptual scheme, such as Role Morality, for linking immediate individual actions to long-range social enterprises. As we shall see in the next chapter, this entails serious difficulties for the Halakhic discussion about social allocation of medical resources.

Notes

1. On all this, see Meyers (1990), 180 ff.

2. cf. Maimonides, MT Evel 14:1. In the Jewish tradition, caring for the dead received the special epithet, "*true* lovingkindness" (*hesed shel emet*), for here alone is the purity of motive finally protected from hopes for reciprocation.

3. According to some writers, this is the reason for the talmudic opinion that a will instructing, "Do not bury me!"

should not be obeyed. Yet the Talmud (BT *sanhedrin* 46b) presents this as a debated and unsettled issue; moreover, it is not clear whose degradation it takes to be at stake.

4. The case was tried only belatedly in 1986 in the Petah Tiqwa Court.

5. See, e.g., Fletcher (1988), pp. 160–64.

6. The surgeon did not, in fact, make any such claim. As he has emphasized to the author (in private communication) and as determined also by the court, he had acted in good faith, erroneously believing that the next of kin had been notified as required by law.

7. The Hebrew term actually includes both incest and adultery. On all this, see BT *sanhedrin* 74a.

8. For a discussion of that epoch, and particularly of the difficulties in the supply of bodies, see Fido (1988).

9. According to Fido (1988, at 3–4), this (lithotomy) was "the sole surgical operation until the nineteenth century. . . . There were no anesthetics . . . many patients died under the operation."

10. I do not know who these rabbis were, nor how the question came to be put before them: was the deceased a Jew, or was perhaps one of the pioneering surgeons/pathologists?

11. See Mishna *yoma* 8:5, and BT *yoma* 83a; and cf. above, Introduction, section I.

12. Emphasis added; this crucial term of Landa's stipulation has been the leading theme in most Halakhic discussions of autopsies. See, e.g., Elon (1969), at 471–72.

13. This remark might be taken as concurrence that a death sentence, as well as pre-mortem consent, can legitimate autopsy. Such a suggestion regarding executed criminals would seem to defy the above-mentioned biblical point of departure; nor is it clear how consent could give license to detract from the divine image. Most subsequent writers in this tradition have maintained that the prohibition, insofar as it is not suspended for the sake of life saving, applies regardless of consent. An exception to this is the position suggested by Rabbi J. Ettlinger, *Binyan Zion* (Altoona, 1868), 170–71.

14. The Hebrew word is *matsuy*, which might be translated also as 'common'. It seems that S. Goren (1980) adopted this alternate reading, although the sequel tends to justify an emphasis on 'present' as opposed to 'future'.

15. The term 'expert knowledge' is a clear reference to the condition for defining a medical emergency which would cause the Shabbat prohibitions to be suspended; cf. Mishna *yoma*, ibid.

16. 'Uziel in fact goes on to argue that there is here, moreover, no violation of respect for the dead, since characterization of an act as disrespectful depends on its motivation. In his view, using a person's body to gain life-saving knowledge brings that person honor rather than degradation.

17. In light of the argument that follows, this prohibition includes apparently even those aiming to save (through new knowledge) a known and present patient. Yet Rosner (1988, at 62 n. 41) presents a more permissive interpretation of Feinstein's position, citing Rosner & Tendler (1980), pp. 67–69. Obviously, life-saving transplantation of cadaver organs should be permitted—indeed required—even by the strictest understanding of Landa's criterion.

18. Compare B. Williams's discussion of the idea that "only an obligation can beat an obligation," which he views as one of the unattractive features of the obligation-centered "morality system" [Williams (1985), at 180].

19. Luban (1988) at 53 (quoting M. Friedman); and cf. a quote to a similar effect from Eshete, at 109.

20. This line of argument is highly reminiscent of R. Feinstein's denial of any special duties pertaining to physicians; all they have is an enhanced duty of life saving defined by their expanded capabilities.

6

Allocating Medical Resources:
Global Planning and Immediate Obligations

I. Treatment versus Medical Progress

In Chapter 4 we examined Feinstein's notion of entitlement, whereby a patient who should have been low on the priority list may, simply by virtue of early arrival, gain an exhaustive claim on limited resources. I offered an explanation for this in terms of a conception of the duty to help as a concrete obligation to a specific individual, as opposed to an abstract obligation of general scope.

This notion of individualized duty seems also to be central in the traditions of the medical profession. The Hippocratic tradition, after all, commits the physician to focus on the welfare of his individual patient.[1] But when we move beyond the micro-level, of "one bed, two patients" addressed by Feinstein, to the issues of allocating resources at macro-levels, we must ask about other, and possibly contrary, obligations. Do health-care providers also have a duty to the public in general? Do they, more precisely, have a duty to dedicate some effort and resources to preparations for treating future patients?

The question is posed most directly in terms of money. Suppose that a finite sum is available for health care,[2] and that it could be spent entirely on curing or sustaining lives of existing patients. Should some part of it be diverted instead to prevention, research, development, and building infrastructure—all aimed at future life saving? Obviously, this question has force mainly where such a diversion is cost-effective, that is, where it is expected to save more people (or also, arguably, more life-years) than would be saved by applying the funds exclusively to immediate treatment.

There is a rough resemblance here to the question addressed by Feinstein at the micro-level. In his view, health-care providers ought in principle to opt for saving the patient with a significantly longer life expectancy. Nevertheless, once they have become committed to another patient with far worse long-term prospects, that patient is said to have acquired an "entitlement" to the available resources, and may not be sacrificed for the sake of greater utility. Might this suggest an analogous social commitment to patients with immediate needs? Can these persons, as a class, claim an entitlement to medical services, leaving no resources free for meeting future needs?

Extending the idea of concrete commitment in this manner seems rather problematic, especially when we consider the most plausible grounds for preferring this notion of commitment and duty over the alternative notion of general, abstract duty. Surely, it is the force of the direct human encounter, the concrete situation, that urges a response and may arguably produce a binding commitment. But there is hardly such a direct encounter supporting a demand to maintain a putatively exhaustive commitment of health-care resources to meeting present needs. It is one thing to forbid removing an individual from intensive care for the sake of greater utility; it is quite another thing to oppose the transfer of funds from intensive care to research expected to save more people.

Still, the claims of future patients are more nebulous than those of the late-arriving claimant for intensive care in Feinstein's discussion. Indeed, as we saw in Chapter 5, Feinstein radically denies that there is a duty upon anyone to acquire or expand capabilities for life saving. Admittedly, this denial comes in the very different context of forestalling an emergency override of prohibitions for the sake of medical research. But ought it not to carry over also to the context of resource allocation?

A clear affirmative answer has been advocated by Feinstein's grandson in law and disciple, S. Rapaport. Citing Feinstein's statement that "One has no duty to acquire knowledge of healing," he concludes:

> creating infrastructure not yet in existence, and likewise [conducting] medical research and development and training physicians in new fields of expertise, *do not constitute a duty* akin to actual life saving. Since in the [presently] obtaining conditions there is no cure for a particular illness—or no infrastructure for transplanting a particular organ—such a patient is in fact untreatable.[3]

Going a step beyond Feinstein, Rapaport does attach some value to enhancing future capabilities, but this value is rather modest. With respect to such a presently "untreatable" patient,

> Generating treatment for his illness is a valuable and worthy[4] enterprise, but not one of actual life saving.
>
> . . . creating medical infrastructure, as well as [conducting] research and development, do not constitute an actual duty. (ibid)

The point is to establish the priority of what is deemed an "actual duty," namely, extending all available modes of life-saving treatment to persons who currently need them. Providing such minimal health care to everyone is, according to Rapaport, an actual and "complete" duty incumbent upon the community, akin to the duty to ensure that every individual has nourishment and clothing sufficient for survival.[5] Therefore,

> If existing resources are not sufficient for [meeting] all needs, the primary duty we have specified takes precedence over the advancement of medicine. The fact that this [primary] duty pertains in great measure to the treatment of the elderly constitutes no reason to curtail or diminish it.[6]

II. Objections on Behalf of Future Patients

Rapaport's position, as initially stated, is extremely conservative, entrenching existing practices and giving low priority to progress. Let us now consider two questions that might be raised regarding his position—one contesting his basic principle and the other pointing to a pragmatic objection.

The first question arises simply by drawing the relevant implication from the view of 'Uziel, who, as we saw in Chapter 5, refuses to limit the notion of 'life saving' to the present context alone. According to 'Uziel, working to obtain medical knowledge is itself required by the duty of life saving, for otherwise "this knowledge will remain forever hidden from us, causing the certain death of several persons." Assuredly, 'Uziel would not advocate ejecting a patient who is already receiving medical care in order to free up resources for research. That would be tantamount to killing him, which is forbidden even for the sake of saving "several lives." But when it comes to allocating resources between current and future life saving, we are, on this view, dealing with a conflict of duties.

It may be retorted that not all duties are of equal force, that the duty to save existing patients is stronger than the duty to provide for curing future ones. Indeed, Rapaport argues not only for the precedence of fulfilling a duty over engaging in the merely "worthy," but also for that of a "greater duty" over a "lesser duty." But the criteria for deciding the relative force of various duties are not entirely clear. Sometimes, in fact, a duty's force appears to be derived from received teachings about its relative precedence, so that we end up with a circular argument.[7]

In the case at hand, however, the conflict is between two instances of the very same duty which, moreover, is generally deemed supreme to virtually all others, that is, life saving. The indicated path would therefore seem to be that of maximizing utility; resources should be allocated in whatever manner is most efficient in terms of lives (or life-years) saved. Against this Rapaport, who is aiming, inter alia, to protect the elderly from threats of "efficient re-allocation," must assert, as indeed he does, that providing for the cure of future patients (or even for enhanced capabilities in treating existing patients) is no duty at all. From this, his argument proceeds, in terms of contemporary ethical discussion, by claiming the primacy of duty over virtue.[8]

As noted above, extending the scope of 'actual duty' beyond the immediate interpersonal encounter is hardly a self-evident move. Let us grant, then, Feinstein's point about the "entitlement" of patients already in treatment. But If more lives can be saved by investing in future capabilities, why not commit any free resources to that and remain simply *unable*, by reason of exhausted resources, to meet any new requests for treatment?

This brings us to the second question, which was put to Rapaport in pragmatic terms by D. Meir, then director of an Orthodox-affiliated hospital in Jerusalem. Meir asks whether Rapaport's advocacy of commitment to present needs would preclude any reshuffling of existing priorities, such as discontinuing expensive units or procedures in favor of greater funding for mundane treatments which could save many more people. Do these conflicting medical endeavors all involve actual duties entailing indissoluble commitments? Meir concludes with a challenging renunciation: "In my view, not everything is a duty!" (Meir, 1992).

Rapaport's response (1992) includes a Halakhic discussion which amounts, in effect, to an admirable effort at setting the limits of present commitments. Unfortunately, Rapaport's full argument is too intricate for exposition in the present framework;[9] instead, we shall look at one illuminating example. Consider a hypothetical policy decision to terminate a program of bypass surgery, motivated by a judgment that it is an inefficient expenditure of resources. It is impermissible, says Rapaport, to announce cancellation of scheduled operations, even if the queue runs for many weeks ahead. But it is legitimate to decide on terminating the program, say, in two years' time, since no person currently in need of bypass surgery can be expected to be still alive and requiring surgery two years hence.

The proffered formulations regarding the proper cutoff are not entirely consistent. What is the status of patients who, when the proposed change comes up for decision, are already in need of the operation but are not yet scheduled or even listed in any queue? At one point, Rapaport implies that they may not be excluded; this seems consistent with his initial insistence on commitment to existing patients. The terms of his formal conclusion, however, seem to protect only those patients who have already been scheduled for treatment.

The issue here is, arguably, not only the need for greater precision in defining the doctrine, but rather—what is more troubling—the doctrine's very coherence, for is there not an endless succession of people in need of any particular treatment? Suppose the termination of bypass surgery is decreed for two years hence. What should be done if a year and ten months later a person is diagnosed as requiring such surgery? Indeed, this person had probably already been in need of the operation for some time; the lack of an earlier diagnosis, and hence also the failure to join the queue, seem merely accidental. If our planned cutoff excludes this person, is it not shown to involve illicitly abandoning an existing patient?

At the heart of these questions lies the murkiness of the grounds for denying a duty of life saving toward future persons. To reiterate 'Uziel's charge, if we know people in the future will need certain resources in order to be treated, why are we not now bound to make those resources available?

III. The Nahmanidean Heritage: Restricting Medical Duty

Feinstein's claim that there is no duty to expand medical capabilities is directed at the individual agent. The rationale for his position, as explicated in Chapter 5, is that the life-saving, cumulative telos of medical research does not readily transfer to the piecemeal contributions of individuals;

hence their actions lack the moral urgency of "life saving."

Rapaport's discussion, however, focuses on the duties of society, for it is society whose funds are to be allocated. True, each of the various options for public expenditure on health care involves a cooperative effort which is carried out by many individuals. But it would be totally misguided to start sorting out the individual actions in the hope of determining the strength of duty attaching to each discrete deed. Rather, social priorities are to be decided in reference to collective enterprises, such as hospital units, research programs, preventive schemes, and the like. Each of these *as a whole* will accomplish a projected measure of life saving; if a lower priority is asserted for those enterprises which consist in efforts to expand capabilities, this calls for a special explanation.

Following up on the analogy to the social duty to provide necessities of life such as food and clothing, the problem becomes even more difficult. Surely those responsible for collection (=taxation) for the public *tzedakah* (=basic welfare) fund must project future needs and make advance arrangements to meet them. Why should preparation for future medical needs be considered less of a duty?

Rapaport is fully conscious of this difficulty and offers an answer which sets medical life saving apart from other modes of life saving. For this, he draws on the Nahmanidean view of medicine as a compromised endeavor. He first cites Maimonides's scathing critique of the Nahmanidean position: ". . . if a person is hungry and seeks bread to eat—whereby he is undoubtedly healed from that great pain—should we say that he has failed to trust in God?!" To this he responds by positing a "fundamental distinction between a person who is drowning or starving [on the one hand] and a sick person [on the other hand]" (p. 15).

> . . . a person afflicted with a potentially fatal illness should not be deemed as a healthy person who needs something and is in lack of it, but rather as one who has started on a path leading to his death. . . .

On account of this difference . . . it could have been argued that humans may not engage in healing the sick, for "God has smitten and it is for Him to heal"; therefore it was necessary for the Torah to grant the physician permission to heal. Nahmanides explains that, once this license has been pronounced, healing comes under the category of 'life-saving'.[10]

Since medical practice is encompassed within the duty of life saving only by virtue of this special license, medical duty is restricted to immediate treatment. We should not, Rapaport suggests, be overly concerned about longer-range responsibilities; whatever illnesses go uncured are the work of God, not for us to undo.

Conclusion: Religious Perspectives and Human Responsibility

Rapaport's discussion is the most sophisticated Halakhic treatment of macro-allocation in health-care that I have come across. Still, his discussion in itself, and the problems we have considered in analyzing it, leave much work to be done, and this chapter is therefore (perhaps disappointingly) rather short. There is not much I can add here on the knotty issues of allocation; instead, let me conclude with an observation of a more general nature.

It is interesting to note that, upon reaching the limits (as he sees them) of the commitment to life saving, a Halakhist like Rapaport falls back on Nahmanidean naturalism. In everyday medical practice, the problematic tenets of religious naturalism generally yield to the imperatives of religious humanism. These imperatives, however, being manifold, produce conflicts amongst themselves. Normally, conflicts in life saving are resolved by exercising deliberate choice and/or following the precepts of individual commitment. Yet sometimes received modes of Halakhic reasoning might seem to call for an abdication of social responsibility. Here the Nahmanidean voice re-emerges, offering a welcome explanation: "This is no dubious abdication, but a pious bowing to divine will."

As suggested by 'Uziel's teaching, the contrary Maimonidean voice calls for the fullest human responsibility. For society at least, duties of life saving include both responding to immediate needs and preparing for the future through the expansion of medical capabilities. Conflicts between these two aspects of life saving cannot be resolved by contrasting the obligatory to the merely virtuous; these categories rightly apply only to individual agents.

Rapaport's own view notwithstanding, the impasse he reaches is not at the limit of human reasoning and responsibility, but only at the limit of received individualistic modes of Halakhic discourse. There is an alternative to falling back on religious naturalism, namely, the challenge of expanding the scope of religious humanism from the individual to the social and political. By contemplating the moral status of institutions, roles, and collective enterprises, we may hope to learn how to extend the range of Halakhic discourse so as to embrace the social and political realities of human existence.

Notes

1. On the Hippocratic tradition, see Veatch (1981), pp. 18–25; Veatch further notes (ibid, at 157) that a competing commitment to medical progress is, in principle, alien to this tradition.

2. In my discussion here I will ignore the grand issue, rightly emphasized by Calabressi & Bobbit (1978), of the overall allocation for health care compared to other areas of spending.

3. Rapaport (1990) at 16; emphasis in the original.

4. The Hebrew term used here is *mitzvah*, which usually means "commandment"; the present context, however, points definitely to the alternate usage, where *mitzvah* in the sense of a (merely) meritorious deed is contrasted to *hova*, a sheer duty.

5. The argument for such a communal duty, and the distinction between it and the obligations incumbent upon individuals, are developed in the same essay (Rapaport, 1990), pp. 10–14.

6. Ibid. at 17. In the following paragraph, the author concludes his essay on an optimistic note, asserting that this order of priorities will in fact not impede medical progress. The necessary resources for research and development and for building medical infrastructure are sure "in any case" to be provided from private (=non-government) sources. Given the role of government funding in research and, in many countries, in building medical infrastructure, this mode of thinking seems more wishful than real.

7. In some of Rapaport's examples, there is a formal difference in the authority behind the duties; in others, however, it seems that we learn which duty is greater by noting which takes precedence. See ibid, pp. 6–8.

8. O. O'neill (1993) argues cogently for thinking of duty and virtue as complementary, rather than as mutually exclusive, modes of ethical discourse. She notes that conflicts are possible within each mode, yet she implies that in a universe of discourse including both modes, the requirements of duty might prevail, in case of conflict, against the guidance of virtue.

9. One interesting point is worth mentioning. Rapaport postulates that it is in general impermissible to reduce people's chances of being rescued. But where this is merely a side effect of action taken in order to save other persons, it is not wrong since, he argues, it does not express a callous attitude toward the loss of human life (ibid at 50).

10. Ibid, pp. 15–16; the reference is to Nahmanides's discussion in his *Torat ha-Adam*, in Vol. 2 in the Chavel edition of Nahmanides's works, p. 49.

References

Primary Sources

For purposes of general reference, I note English translations when such have been published, but all citations in the book are in my own translation.

Babylonian Talmud [=BT]. Complete English translation, edited by I. Epstein. London: Soncino, 1935–52.

Mishnah [=Mishna]. Translated by H. Danby. Oxford: Clarendon Press, 1933.

Mekilta de-Rabbi Ishmael [=Mekhilta]. Translated by J. Z. Lauterbach. Philadelphia: JPS, 1933, 1961.

Maimonides. *Commentary to the Mishna.* The original Arabic text, along with a fine Hebrew translation by J. Kapah, was published by Jerusalem: Mosad ha-Rav Kook, 1963–68.

—— *Mishneh Torah* [=MT]. English translation, L. Nemoy, general editor, *The Code of Maimonides*, New Haven: Yale University Press (Yale Judaica Series), 1949.

Nahmanides. *Commentary to the Torah.* Translated by B. Chavel, New York: Shilo Press, 1971–76.

—— *Kitvey ha-Ramban* [=The Works of Nahmanides, Hebrew]. Edited by B. Chavel. Jerusalem: Mosad Harav Kook, 1963–64.

R. Joseph Caro. *Bet Yoseph.* Printed in the standard editions of R. Jacob ben Asher's code, *Arba'a Turim.*

—— *Shulhan 'Arukh,* Caro's concise summary of his encyclopedic *Bet Yoseph.* Citations in this book to both these works of Caro, and to the accompanying glosses by *rema* (R. Moshe Isserlish), refer to the section *yore de'a*, abbreviated as YD.

Other Works

Beauchamp, T.L. (1976). "An Analysis of Hume's Essay 'On Suicide'," *Review of Metaphysics* 30, 73–95.

Ben-Shim'on, R.A. (1908). *Nehar Mitsrayim* (in Hebrew), Alexandria.

Berkovits, E. (1983). *Not in Heaven*, New York: Ktav.

Bleich, J.D. (1977–89). *Contemporary Halakhic Problems*, Vol. I–III. New York: Ktav.

Bleich, J.D. and Rosner, F., editors (1983). *Jewish Bioethics* (Second Edition). New York: Hebrew Publishing Company.

Brandt, R.B. (1980). "The Rationality of Suicide," reprinted in Battin, M.P. & Mayo, D.J., editors, *Suicide: the Philosophical Issues*. New York: St. Martin's Press, (117–32).

Brody, B.A. (1983). "The Use of Halakhic Material in Discussions of Medical Ethics," *Journal of Medicine and Philosophy* 8, 317–28.

Cahn, E.N. (1955). *The Moral Decision*. Bloomington: Indiana University Press.

Calabressi, G. and Bobbit, P. (1978). *Tragic Choices*. New York: Norton.

Chadwick, R., editor (1987). *Ethics, Reproduction and Genetic Control*. London: Croom Helm.

Childress, J.F. (1983). "Who Shall Live When Not All Can Live?" reprinted in S. Gorovitz et al., editors, *Moral Problems in Medicine*, Second Edition. New Jersey: Prentice-Hall, 640–49.

Ciesielski-Carlucci, C. & Kimsma, G. (1994). "A Report from the Netherlands," *Bioethics* 8 (2), 151–58.

Daube, D. (1965). *Collaboration with Tyranny in Rabbinic Law*. London: Oxford University Press.

Davis, D.S. (1991). "Beyond Rabbi Hiyya's Wife: Women's Voices in Jewish Bioethics," *Second Opinion* 16 (March), 10–30.

——— (1994). "Method in Jewish Bioethics," in P.F. Camenisch, editor, *Religious Methods and Resources in Bioethics*. Boston: Kluwer Academic.

Dickenson, D. (1991). *Moral Luck in Medical Ethics and Practical Politics*. Aldershot: Avebury.

Dikhovsky, S. (1976). "Precedence and Priorities in Rescuing Lives According to Halakha" (in Hebrew), *Diney Yisrael 7*, 45–66.

Dorff, E.N (1991a). "A Jewish Approach to End-Stage Medical Care," *Conservative Judaism 43*, 3–51.

―――― (1991b), "A Methodology for Jewish Medical Ethics," *Jewish Law Association Studies*, Vol. 7, 35–57.

Dratch, M. (1990). "His Money or Her Life? Heinz's Dilemma in Jewish Law," *Journal of Halacha and Contemporary Society* XX, 111–29.

Dworkin, R. (1993). *Life's Dominion*. New York: Knopf.

Elon, M. (1969). "Jewish Law and Modern Medicine," *Israel Law Review 4*, 467–78.

―――― (1994). *Jewish Law: history, sources, principles*, Auerbach, B. and Sykes, M.J., translators. Philadelphia: Jewish Publication Society

Falk, Z. (1962). *Jewish Matrimonial Law in the Middle Ages*. Oxford: Oxford University Press.

Feldman, D.M. (1968, 1974). *Marital Relations, Birth Control and Abortion in Jewish Law*. New York: Schocken.

―――― (1986). *Health and Medicine in the Jewish Tradition*. New York: Crossroad.

Fido, M. (1988). *Bodysnatchers: A History of the Resurrectionists, 1742–1832*. London: Weidenfeld & Nicolson.

Fletcher, G. (1988). *A Crime of Self Defence: Bernard Geotz and the Law on Trial*. New York: MacMillan.

Gereboff, J. (1982). "Jewish Bioethics: Redefining the Field," *Religious Studies Review* 8(4), 316–24.

Go'elman, Y. (1984). "Saul's Death as Reflected in Halakhic Literature" (in Hebrew), in *'Arakhim be-Mivhan Milhama*. Jerusalem, 233–51.

Gold, M. (1988). *And Hannah Wept: Infertility, Adoption, and the Jewish Couple.* Philadelphia: Jewish Publication Society.

Goldstein, S. (1989). *Suicide in Rabbinic Literature,* Hoboken: Ktav.

Goren, S. (1980). "Studying Anatomy in Medical Schools" (in Hebrew), *Me'orot* 2, 5–17.

Graetz, M. (1991). "The Right to Medical Treatment—Ethics and Halakha" (in Hebrew), *'Et La'asot* 3, 80–89.

Green, R.M. (1985). "Contemporary Jewish Bioethics: A Critical Assessment," in E.E. Shelp, editor, *Theology and Bioethics.* Dordrecht: D. Reidel, 245–66.

Ha-Levi, H.D. (1981). "Disconnecting a Terminal Patient from an Artificial Respirator," *Techumin* II, 297–305.

Halperin, M. (1985), editor. *Emek Halachah—Asya:* A collection of Articles Relating to Physicians and Medicine in Halachah, Jerusalem (in Hebrew).

Hare, R.M. (1952). *The Language of Morals.* Oxford: Clarendon Press.

Harris, J. (1975). "The Survival Lottery," *Philosophy* 50, 81–87.

Hartman, D. (1985). *A Living Covenant: The Innovative Spirit in Traditional Judaism.* New York: Free Press.

Herring, B.F. (1984). *Jewish Ethics and Halakha for Our Time.* New York: Ktav.

Herschler, M. (1981). "The Obligation to Rescue Sick People and Those in Danger" (Hebrew), *Halakhah u-Refu'ah* 2. Jerusalem: Regenshberg Institute, 29–43.

Heyd, D. (1992). *Genethics: Moral Issues in the Creation of People.* Berkeley: University of California Press.

Holly, D.M. (1989). "Voluntary Death, Property Rights, and the Gift of Life," *The Journal of Religious Ethics* 17(1), 103–21.

Hume, D. (reprinted 1875). "Of Suicide," in his *Essays,* Vol. II. Green, T.H. and Grose, T.H., editors. London, 406–14.

Jacobs, J. (1982). *The Moral Justification of Suicide.* Springfield: Charles Thomas.

Jakobovits, I. (1975). *Jewish Medical Ethics*. New York: Bloch.

Jellinek, A. (1853). *Bet ha-Midrash* (in Hebrew). Leipzig.

Kamm, F.M. (1985). "Equal Treatment and Equal Chances," *Philosophy and Public Affairs* 14(2), 177–94.

—— (1993). *Morality, Mortality*, Vol. 1: Death and Whom To Save from It. New York: Oxford University Press.

Kellner, M. (1987). "Reflections on the Impossibility of Jewish Ethics," *Bar Ilan Annual* 32–33. Ramat Gan: Bar Ilan University Press, English section [45]–[52].

Klein, I. (1979). *A Guide to Jewish Religious Practice*. New York: Jewish Theological Seminary.

Leiman, S.Z. (1983). "Therapeutic Homicide: A Philosophic and Halakhic Critique of Harris' 'Survival Lottery'," *Journal of Medicine and Philosophy* 8 (3), 257–67.

Lichtenberg, J. (1982). "The Moral Equivalence of Action and Omission," reprinted in Steinbock and Norcross (1994), 210–29.

Luban, D. (1988). *Lawyers and Justice*. Princeton: Princeton University Press.

McMahan, J. (1993). "Killing, Letting Die, and Withdrawing Aid," reprinted in Steinbock and Norcross (1994), 383–420.

—— (1994). "Self-Defense and the Problem of the Innocent Attacker," *Ethics* 104.

Meier, L., editor (1986). *Jewish Values in Bioethics*. New York: Human Sciences Press.

Meir, D. (1992). "Priorities in Allocating Public Resources to Medicine," *Asya* 51–52, 185–86.

Meisel, A. (1995). *The Right to Die*, 2nd edition. New York: J. Wiley.

Meyers, D.W. (1990). *The Human Body and the Law*, Second Edition. Edinburgh: Edinburgh University Press.

Morrell, S. (1982). "An Equal or a Ward: How Independent is a Married Woman According to Rabbinic Law?" *Jewish Social Studies* 44, 189–210.

Newman, L.A. (1990). "Woodchoppers and Respirators: The Problem of Interpretation in Contemporary Jewish Ethics," *Modern Judaism* 10, 17–42.

——— (1993). "Talking Ethics with Strangers: A View from the Jewish Tradition," *Journal of Medicine and Philosophy* 18, 549–67.

Novak, D. (1985). "Judaism and Contemporary Bioethics," in *Halakha in a Theological Dimension*. California: Scholars Press, 82–101.

——— (1992). *The Theology of Nahmanides Systematically Presented*. Atlanta: Scholars Press.

O'neill, O. (1993). "Duties and Virtues," in A.P. Griffiths, editor, *Ethics*. Royal Institute of Philosophy Supplement 35. Cambridge: Cambridge University Press, 107–20.

Pool, D. Di-Sola (1916). "Capital Punishment Among the Jews," in *Jewish Eugenics and Other Essays*. New York: Bloch, 51–103.

Rackman, E. (1986). "Priorities in the Right to Life," in Sacks, J., editor, *Tradition and Transition*, London, 235–44.

Ramsey, P. (1970). *The Patient as Person: Explorations in Medical Ethics*. New Haven: Yale University Press.

Rapaport, S. ha-Kohen (1990). "Priorities in Allocating Public Resources in Medicine," *Asya* 49–50, 5–17.

——— (1992). "Priorities in Allocating Public Resources to Medicine—in the Wake of Professor Meir's Comments." *Asya* 51–52, 46–53.

Rosner, F. (1983a). "Allocation of Scarce Medical Resources— The Jewish View," *New York State Journal of Medicine* (March), 353.

——— (1983b). "The Rationing of Medical Care: The Jewish View," *Journal of Halacha and Contemporary Society* VI, 21–32.

——— (1988). "Skin Grafting and Skin Banks in Jewish Law," *Journal of Halacha and Contemporary Society* XV, 53–65.

Rosner, F. and Tendler, M.D. (1980). *Practical Medical Halacha*. New York: Raphael Society.

Sandel, M. (1982). *Liberalism and the Limits of Justice*. Cambridge: Cambridge University Press.

Sagi, A. and Statman, D. (1995). "Divine Command Morality in Jewish Tradition," *Journal of Religious Ethics* 23, 39–67.

Scheffler, S. (1982). *The Rejection of Consequentialism*. Oxford: Clarendon Press.

Shalev, C. (1989). *Birth Power*. New Haven: Yale University Press.

Singer, M.G. (1961). *Generalization in Ethics*. New York: Knopf.

Sinclair, D.B. (1989). *Tradition and the Biological Revolution*. Edinburgh: Edinburgh University Press.

Snowden, R., Mitchell, G.D., and Snowden, E.M. (1983). *Artificial Reproduction: A Social Investigation*. London: George Allen and Unwin.

Steinberg, A. (1988). *Encyclopedia of Medicine and Jewish Law* (in Hebrew). Jerusalem: Shlesinger Institute (English translation by F. Rosner in progress, expected publication 1998–99).

Steinbock, B. and Norcross, A., editors (1994). *Killing and Letting Die* (Second Edition). New York: Fordham University Press.

Taurek, J.M. (1977). "Should the Numbers Count?" *Philosophy and Public Affairs* 6(4), 293–316.

Toledano, P. (1986). "A Responsum on Issues of Medical Halakhah," in *Tradition and Transition*, J. Sacks, editor. London: Jews' College, Hebrew section, i–xv.

Twersky, I. (1972). *A Maimonides Reader*. New York: Behrman House.

Twycross, R.G. (1981). "Voluntary Euthanasia," in S.E. Wallace and A. Eser, editors, *Suicide and Euthanasia*. Knoxville: University of Tennessee Press, 88–98.

Veatch, R.M. (1981). *A Theory of Medical Ethics*. New York: Basic Books.

Walzer, M. (1973). "Political Action: The Problem of Dirty Hands," reprinted in M. Cohen et al., editors, *War and Moral Responsibility*, Princeton University Press, 1974, 62–82.

———— (1992). "The Legal Codes of Ancient Israel," *Yale Journal of Law and the Humanities* 4 (2), 335–49.

Warnock, M. (1985). *A Question of Life: The Warnock Report on Human Fertilisation and Embryology.* Oxford: Basil Blackwell.

Weiss-Halivni, D. (1986). *Midrash, Mishnah and Gemara: The Jewish Predilection for Justified Law.* Cambridge: Harvard University Press.

Williams, B.O. (1971). "The Idea of Equality," in *Justice and Equality*, H.A. Bedau, editor, Englewood Cliffs: Prentice-Hall, 116–37.

———— (1980). *Ethics and the Limits of Philosophy.* Cambridge: Harvard University Press.

Wueste, D.E. (1991). "Taking Role Moralities Seriously," *The Southern Journal of Philosophy* 29(3), 407–16.

Zohar, N. (1991). "Prospects for 'Genetic Therapy': Can a Person Benefit from Being Altered?," *Bioethics* 4, 275–88.

———— (1993a). "Marriage as Acquisition and the Religious Subservience of Women," in *Approaches to Ancient Judaism* (N.S., Vol. V), H. Basser and S. Fishbane, editors, Atlanta: Scholars Press, 33–54.

———— (1993b). "Collective War and Individualistic Ethics: Against the Conscription of 'Self-Defense'," *Political Theory* 21, 606–22.

———— (1993c). "Human Beings as Divine Possessions—On the Trend of Halachic Opposition to Euthanasia" (in Hebrew), in D. Statman and A. Sagi, editors, *Religion and Morality*, Ramat Gan: Bar-Ilan University Press, 145–56.

Index

Note: Name of Halakhic work follows author's name in parenthesis where the author is better known by work.